Uncommon Sense

Finding Your Voice
Among The Noise

Brysen Johnson

Courronne Publishing
Winnipeg, Manitoba

Copyright © 2017 by Brysen Johnson.

All rights reserved. No part of this publication may be reproduced, distributed or transmitted in any form or by any means, including photocopying, recording, or other electronic or mechanical methods, without the prior written permission of the publisher, except in the case of brief quotations embodied in critical reviews and certain other noncommercial uses permitted by copyright law. For permission requests, write to the publisher, addressed "Attention: Permissions Coordinator," at the address below:

Couronne publishing Inc.
Info@couronnepublishing.com
www.couronnepublishing.com

Book Cover by: Vanessa Mendozzi
Front Cover image by: Uri Portillo

Ordering Information:
Quantity sales. Special discounts are available on quantity purchases by corporations, associations, and others. For details, contact the "Special Sales Department" at the address above.

Uncommon Sense/ Brysen Johnson. —1st ed.
ISBN: 978-1-988497-02-0

Contents

Introduction 7

Where it all started 11

A different path 19

Facing fears... 29

The belief... 35

Decluttering.. 47

Living life for yourself 55

Patience is key.. 63

Learning along the way....................................... 73

Stopping the chase 83

The truth revealed 95

A day of loss... 103

New Beginnings.. 115

Break the Silence.. 121

Bonus.. 127

Bonus

As a special bonus for readers of this book, I'm offering you access to a special Mini course on "Finding your voice"

To Access this mini course, register your book at <u>www.brysenjohnson.com/bonus</u>

This book is dedicated to my grandmother Antonietta Perillo, and my grandfather Simbi Johnson who both passed away in 2016, for their unwavering love, support, and instilling with me the strength I needed to write this book. To my mother Franca, and my father Bill for always believing in me and teaching me the value of hard work, while being the best parents I could ever ask for. To my sister Tara for her unconditional love and support and being the best sister a brother could have. To my many aunts, uncles, and cousins who have always been there for me to keep me grounded and appreciated. To the friends who have stuck by me through thick and thin, who have always had my back, you know who you are.

Introduction

We can bring forward with us in life a knowledge to become better for ourselves, and the people around us. Whether it's a good experience or bad, we can always find something within it to teach us something new. I have learned that in order for myself, and anyone else for that matter, to become happier more uplifted people we must experience an immense amount of pain. Sometimes this pain will be physical, other times it will be emotional. Through pain we find strength, and that's what I want to give to you within these pages, a chance for my pain to become your strength. To help you realize that there is no right or wrong way to live life, especially as a young adult coming up in the world.

The stories in this book and the words I speak, are meant to be taken as educational tools to help guide you through the trial and errors of life. I am not perfect, and as a young man I made many mistakes in my life. By sharing these experiences with you, I hope to show you that it's ok to make mistakes. It's ok to fail at things while you are finding your way in life. The point of every single experience we go through is for it to teach us something.

We are all going to make tremendously large mistakes; we are all going to suffer enormous blows to our ego. It is necessary in order for us to become who we were meant to be. Everyone who reads this book can come to a realization within themselves, that it is possible to make many mistakes and still come out on top. That trying many different things in life and messing up, not being happy, failing and everything else that comes with it, will be the stepping stones to a better life.

I had a hard time standing up for myself as a kid, and as I grew older it became even harder to step up and tell the world off. Through the experiences I went through and the music I fought so hard to play, I found my voice. This would have never happened if I quit too soon. I found my confidence and discovered abilities that I did not know I was capable of doing. Everything in this book comes from the heart; the stories shared are some that I have never shared publicly before. I want these pages to shed a light on my life that few people have ever seen. Allowing everyone out there to realize they have to find their voice in life. As well, to not let anyone or anything stop you from achieving your dreams. Thank you for giving me the opportunity to share my life with you. Cheers to finding your voice.

CHAPTER 1

Where it all started

As a young man, I knew right from the start of my life that I was somewhat different than other kids. I ate different food, I talked about different things, I found things funnier than others did. I never thought of myself as weird or different, until people started telling me I was. Those words hurt, and cut me deep more often than not. I never really understood the word weird. Did it mean I was dumb? No. Did it mean I had some sort of disability? Not at all. It meant people did not understand me. And throughout my life, that would be a recurring factor that led me to the biggest successes I could ever have.

People look at you differently, and make you feel like an outsider when you are considered weird. But what is so wrong about being an outsider? For a young kid, there is a lot wrong with feeling like you don't fit in and really not feeling included. Feeling left out, or not invited to things made me upset and unsure of myself. It made me doubt if I had any real value to offer people. I literally felt worthless because I thought no one wanted me around and was treated as such. I have always enjoyed being around people, so when a birthday party invite never came, not being included in a night out with friends, or not being picked to be on a team with someone in gym class, I was hurt. Kids my age were constantly criticizing me as well. I wasn't a particularly liked individual as a kid, so to take myself out of the spotlight, I would divert all attention from myself, and become a shadow on the wall. It's sad if you think about it; we become so worried about how others will judge us that we become someone who does not embody our personality, and mannerisms. Becoming something and someone different, to please others and not upset the status quo.

We learn from a young age that in order to be left alone, and avoid harsh criticism, we must embody what is the least likely object of ridicule. We start becoming different people because that's the role we need to play in order to get through growing up. It's like a stupid game no one wants to be a part of, yet everyone needs to play. Maybe not everyone felt this way, but to me I saw myself having to change my entire persona in order for people to stay away from me. I had to become colder, disinterested, a completely different person from who I was. Eventually with time, I learned that it did not matter how I acted, people will always find a way to judge you. But at the time, it seemed like the only way to avoid confrontation was to completely change, inside and out. With an intent to avoid any and all friction with people in order to keep the hateful eyes off of us, and onto something or someone different. We don't necessarily care if those eyes are piercing and hurting someone else, just as long as we aren't the ones feeling that burn.

When I was in high school, I remember the first day I came to school dressed in completely new clothes I had never worn before. At this time, slim fitting jeans on guys were not a popular item of choice. I remember the first time I saw an older kid in school wearing them and thought they were the coolest things. Although they were just pants, I have always been mesmerized and drawn to things that held a unique and outstanding quality to them. So, I had to grab myself a pair. Through friends at school, I heard about a local thrift shop that sold these slim fitting jeans, that were hard to come by at the time. See, back in the day, I couldn't just walk into the mall and find any old skate shop and pick myself up a pair of nice slim fitting jeans. I had to drive to the nearest thrift shop with my mom. There was a search and rescue mission happening in this store, and I wanted my own pair badly. After an hour of searching, I finally found what I was looking for. They were black jeans, made out of a stretchy material, and one of the most comfortable pairs of pants that I have ever worn in my life. I was so excited, checking myself out in the mirror like I was getting ready for some lame school dance, I could not wait to wear them to school the next day.

I had no idea what exactly I thought was going to happen when I wore these pants to school for the first time. I must have been thinking very little, or very naïve. Either way, I went to school not expecting much of anything. Maybe a few turned heads, a few compliments, and on with my day I would go. Boy was I wrong and I found that out the moment I stepped into the cafeteria that day. Only a few feet inside the doorway of the cafeteria, I began hearing laughter from kids around me, snickering at my legs and new look. One kid I had known for years walked up to me and began picking out things he hated about my outfit. From my shirt, my sweater, to the brand-new jeans I was so excited to wear. It was one of the most embarrassing moments of my life, like having my entire happiness that day stripped away with every piece of clothing he mocked. Any confidence I may have had while wearing these pants instantly was destroyed. To this day, I still don't understand why I was picked out of the handful of kids that wore the same style of clothes. Just my luck I guess.

The teasing only got worse as I went through that awful day. Kids who were lined up in the halls waiting outside of classrooms for their teachers pointed and laughed at me while I walked past them. Literally groups of 50 kids stared at me, mocking and laughing as I kept my head down and pretended not to pay attention. I could feel a lump in my throat, and butterflies in my stomach. Feeling like a piece of trash everyone wanted to take a swing at, I couldn't understand why I was getting this type of treatment. For some reason, I kept wearing the pants. Every day, I would come to school wearing them. I eventually bought a few more pairs. Then got my mom to hem a few old jeans into slim fitting ones, and continued pissing people off. It was hard—really hard, having kids constantly mock me. And sometimes they were so blatantly obvious, it made me want to smack them with my books. I remember one particular incident where I was standing beside a friend during the lunch period in the cafeteria, wearing a pair of tight blue jeans I had recently purchased. A girl sitting at a table nearby had been making fun of me amongst her friends. I didn't realize it, until she stood up, walked over to where I was standing, and began posing beside me to emphasize the similarities between our two pairs of pants. Her friends burst into laughter, as she stood proudly beside me. I have never been one for confrontation, so instead of standing up for myself, I slowly moved away from her as though I had not noticed a thing. That one stung pretty badly and to this day, it's still a memory that bugs me a bit. Not because I was made fun of, but because I never stood up for myself and told those kids off.

The ongoing joke was that my pants looked as though I had bought them from a girl's clothing store. Many kids at my age who had worn that style of jeans had to resort to girl jeans. They were the only kind of pants that fit in the style they were looking for. I was proud enough to say I never resorted to wearing girl's jeans, despite many kids who believed I did, and mocked me for that fact. Throughout this entire ordeal, I began realizing I was letting the fear of criticism dictate my actions.

One summer I refused to wear anything slim on my legs, I had had enough of the name calling, and abuse that was being given to me by kids I had no intention of learning more about me. I literally spent more time in my house than I would in public in fear of running into one of those bullies from school. I felt ashamed of myself and the choice I had made to put myself in the spot light of ridicule. It was my own fault I know, but I felt awful for being hurt by so many people based off of my looks. I soon realized how dumb I felt for constantly feeling ashamed of these stupid pairs of jeans. And realized I was not enjoying wearing them only because these kids made feel bad for doing so. It was then that I made up my mind the following school year to continue wearing the jeans. The jokes came and went, but eventually, people got tired of giving me a hard time.

I soon came to the realization that most, if not all people, are hypocrites in one way or another. One particular kid at my school had given me a hard time the most out of everyone. He tormented me every time I walked down the hall. It was as though he was everywhere at the same time, constantly around the corner waiting to take a chunk out of me.

"Are those girl jeans?" he'd mockingly yell at me, always trying to intimidate and criticize me in front of his friends. He was a year older, yet the year I was supposed to graduate, he had stayed back after failing so many classes. I began wearing my new look during the beginning of the 10th grade; one of the worst years of my high school life. By the 12th grade, I still wore the same pair of jeans. But to make the situation hilarious, the kid who had tormented me for the past two years, had begun wearing tighter jeans than mine. This kid made my life a living hell at school, and he became a walking hypocrite. It proved to me a few things; people are always going to have something to criticize you for, and if you let every single negative person take a chunk of your happiness, you will live a sad lonely life. It proved that if you stay true to the values you hold yourself to, and stay strong through adversity, eventually the negativity will dissipate. And those who once mocked you profusely, will start following in your footsteps. Funny how a pair of pants can actually teach you a few life lessons. I still wear the same style of pants to this day, but this time around, I wear them with my head held high.

CHAPTER 2

A different path

We all have a little voice inside of our heads telling us "this is the wrong choice" when thinking about what to do with our lives. An inner battle with ourselves often occurs on whether or not we want to pursue something that will dictate our life for the next 40 years or more. Young kids growing up in junior high and high school are particularly experienced in the skill of over thinking. From the time we have reached puberty, every adult around us has begun the awful process of sharing their life wisdom, in order to help us succeed in the world. The words "you can be anything you want to be" become a backburner statement, replaced by "you better start thinking about what degree you want to study for, school you want to attend, and job you want to do for the rest of your life".

Most young kids have no idea what they want to do with the rest of their lives, they barely have a clue as to what they want to do on the weekend. It's an incredibly frustrating situation growing up, constantly being given advice we don't want, by people who are just trying to help. When my 12th grade year began, the pressure to start figuring out my life was in high gear. The keeners of every class were on high alert for any and every opportunity to push their grades higher, to join more extra-curricular activities, anything to enhance their college and university applications. At the time, these kids made me sick. They stressed themselves out to the point of near insanity. They began having mental breakdowns if their classmate got a 99% while they came out with a 98.5%. I was a below average student, not that I wasn't smart, I was just completely uninterested in the topics being taught to me. English class was the only subject where I succeeded. It was the easiest for me, I've always had a way with using my imagination to paint a picture with words. Once even getting the top mark in my grade for a mid-term English exam, I always had an easy time with the language arts. When I saw the over achievers losing their minds over not getting a perfect grade, I resented them and bugged them for it. Many of these people went on to do amazing things in their educational lives but during high school, I hated anything to do with them and school.

When we began learning how to apply to university, and what classes schools would be looking at in order for us to have the best chance to be accepted, I couldn't have cared less. My mind was not interested in focusing on my future. If it involved school, I wanted no part of it. As a lazy kid, I had no intention to go back to school. After spending the last 13 years of life imprisoned by the shackles of education, I was exhausted and done with it. My parents constantly asked me what I wanted to do with my life.

"What career interests you most?" they asked, as though I would have a clue at the age of 17. "Touring musician?" I would say jokingly, but also in a quite serious way as well. Knowing full well how serious I was about that statement, but never admitting it to my parents.

I was in love with music, a feeling that began at a young age. When I was 11, I remember walking into the band room of my old elementary school. The 8th grade class was practicing for the upcoming school band concert. Every year, the junior high classes performed for the teachers, students, and parents for a few hours, a couple times a year. Watching the drummer playing through his band's songs, I was mesmerized by what I was seeing. He was playing with so much passion, so much energy, I had never heard or seen an instrument played like that before. I spent the whole class watching the drummer play, the banging of the drums was like tasting pizza for the first time; amazingly beautiful, and something I have never forgotten.

After that day, I decided I wanted to be a drummer. Every lunch break, I stayed after band class and fiddled around on the drum set. I was in love with this instrument the more I played it. I wasn't a child prodigy by any means, but I was so happy every time I sat down behind the kit, I didn't care how bad I was. A lot of my classmates had a hard time seeing my passion for the drums as a particularly good thing. Mocking me as much as they could, I was told more times than not to get off the drums, that I sucked, and many other lovely hurtful words. I didn't care, I continued doing my lunch time solo jam sessions in the band room until my band teacher began taking notice in my particular passion for the instrument. During a parent teacher conference, later in the year, my band teacher informed my parents about what I had been up to every lunch hour.

"So, that's why you haven't been coming home" my dad joked. His lunch hour at work always matched up with mine, so he had been confused when I began not coming home from school during that time. My teacher talked my parent's ears off about my new-found love of the drums, and spoke highly about the idea of getting my own drum set at home.

"If you can prove to us you are really interested, in a year's time, we will buy you your own drum set," my dad promised. The deal was, I had to take drum lessons for a year, and I would rent a drum set. If I could prove to them I was committed to learning, they would have no problem buying my own drum set. So, with that being said, I signed up for drum lessons, picked up my first drum set, and began practicing every day that I could.

When you're truly passionate about something in life, hard work is never really part of the equation. It's never work when you enjoy it, it's never hard when you are truly interested in it. Spending every day on the drum set was the best thing I could do with my time, because my heart and head were always in it. The following school year, I came to band class determined to show all those kids who had made fun of me what I could do. I set myself up on the drums, and began to play. All of a sudden, kids who hated the sight of me on the drum set, now didn't want me to stop playing. Suddenly they wanted me to join bands with them. I knew at that point, I had made the right choice to stay true to what I loved. The hard work paid off; a valuable lesson I would take with me for the rest of my life.

So when my adult life came around, I knew my choice was made up. I wanted to travel the world and become a professional musician. However, I wasn't looking to become a rock star, it made me happy enough playing small 200 person venues each night. Anything that got in the way of my own dream was not worth my time. When I got my first job at a grocery store, I hated the fact that I had to take time away from music to go do something I hated. When the idea of going to university came up and I was forced to choose between full time school, or trying to tour with my band. I put my whole life on hold for my dream, and whether it was a smart thing to do or not, I knew what I wanted in my life. I had found a passion and I wasn't going to waiver from it whatsoever.

It's hard holding onto a dream when everything around you is telling you to waiver from it. It's hard staying positive and optimistic when everyone is telling you your dreams are stupid, and not worth your time. My parents favorite line was "remember, music is just a hobby". They were right, but I didn't feel that way. I was determined to do something bigger in my life than to just go to school, get a job, and settle into adult life without at least trying my best to get somewhere. When graduation came, the ceremony was like sitting through a Great Uncle showing you a slide show of his favorite plants, and your parents are making you go through it. I didn't want to go to my grad ceremony, I was in a position where I had very few people I was close to, and I had no interest in spending one more day with any of them. My least favorite part was sitting through the awards. For anyone who's an underachiever like I was in school, watching all the know it all, keener kids go up and get award after award was pretty sickening. They could have taken a chunk of the ceremony and turned it into a presentation on why this group of overachievers was so great, how much money in scholarships they were going to be getting, and how much brighter their future was going to be compared to the rest of us. It felt that way to me, and as I watched these kids walk up and accept their prizes, I felt a sick feeling in my stomach. Not only because I felt like I could have done more, but because I felt bad for my parents, knowing their son could have done more with his time in school.

I don't think it's many parent's dream to have a son who's aspiring to be a professional homeless person. My parents never really understood why I wanted to put my entire life on hold in order to do something big with music. Time after time they would push new and creative ideas for me to get a better job, go after something different in school, do anything that wasn't playing music. They supported me and my dreams as best as they could, but at a certain point they had had enough.

After graduation from high school, I began working more hours. Nothing full time, just enough to keep me and my very few bills afloat. Remember, I was a lazy suburban kid who wanted to become a touring musician. Money was of no concern at the time because it had nothing to do with what I wanted with my life. My parents taught me the value of hard work, but pushed away the idea of going after something you are passionate about, when the results were unrealistic. They were incredibly supportive of me, but wanted to make sure I was in the best possible position to succeed in life.

When you are going after something bigger for your life, you're going to be met with a lot of criticism. A lot of people will not understand you, nor will they make an effort to do so. My biggest struggle growing up was learning how to deal with the consequences of following my own path. I was not going to fit in with the rest of the kids I went to school with. My family was supportive, but could not understand why I would want to chase a dream, rather than create a life of stability for myself. You have to learn to chase your dream without people supporting you, or understanding you. You will have to deal with a lot of harsh criticism for a very long time. A lot of people will not want to see you succeed. They will not want to watch you throw your life away, in their opinion, you are wasting valuable time. If you listen to everyone else's opinions about your own life, you will never truly accomplish what you want to with your own life. You will be living a life that is not your own, a life for other people, and that's the biggest waste of your energy you will ever go through.

Following the path of least resistance may be the easiest, but it is filled with the most unsatisfied people. I learned throughout my whole life to listen to my heart, and my gut; to take judgment on my goals lightly. Also, to always remember that I am doing something bigger for myself, not so others will accept me. You must become your own best friend in these tough times, it will be lonely and you will feel like there's something wrong with you. Keep pushing through, keep striving for more, there's no doubt in my mind you can achieve anything you want if you're willing to stick it out through the crap life throws at you.

CHAPTER 3

Facing fears

Growing up is tough, as a young adult you learn a lot about the world far too quickly to get a real grasp of it. I had just graduated from high school, and was working a job selling shoes with my best friend. Pursuing music was my passion, and I thought about it day in and day out. The job my friend and I worked at was easy, we could spend time writing music in the back of the store while business was slow. We had a great set up and it worked out well for us. Both of us were in the same boat, he was a year older, but was already feeling the pressure of not knowing what he wanted to do with his life. We both wondered why we were the ones not going to school, while everyone else seems to be figuring their lives out? We both knew music was something we loved, and being realistic, we probably were not going to make a living at. It was nice having someone who could relate to avoiding any and all traditional milestones as a young man, and choosing to be irresponsible for a while.

We didn't know it at the time, but we were making progress. We were perhaps taking longer to figure our stuff out, but by working jobs we hated, we realized what we didn't want to do for the rest of our lives. It was a blessing in disguise, even if it didn't feel like it. I had a lot of fun back in those days, because I truly was living an easy life. With no real responsibilities, I rarely thought about my future in a constructive way, and would instead silently worry about it but continue not to change it. My dreams outweighed my lack of money, and real prospects of a secure future. I felt good about chasing something so exciting, but embarrassed to admit that I was worried at the same time.

Whether we liked admitting it or not, money had to become a concern when pursuing things in our lives because, damn, were we broke. I always felt like an outsider, watching the world around me moving faster and faster, while I was standing still. Many friends had begun their post-secondary education, and I was working part time at a shoe store. My band was not doing much at this time, and I felt pretty useless. My parents always warned me about working with people who did not have the same ambitions for music as I did. I was pushing a dead horse for many years of my life. Although I learned many things, and experienced a lot, the price I paid was a tough one to swallow. More on that later.

The first few years after high school were a bit of a messy blur. I had no idea what I was doing, but I knew I wasn't completely happy. My friends and I would spend our weekends and any other night we could either playing shows, or going to local bands shows and hanging out at Boston Pizza. It was a really fun time for me, as I had never had a chance to truly have that freedom in high school. I had a solid group of real friends for a change and we spent as much time as we could together. But the idea of figuring out my life was always a bit of a concern. It was a constant worry, but something I always buried in the back of my mind and tried to forget about.

It didn't help that my parents were constantly on my back to work more hours and start thinking about school. The more they nagged, the harder I pushed back. I could never figure out why I wasn't getting what everyone else was. I knew I should be going to school, but I really didn't know why. Was it because everyone else around me was doing it? Yes. Social proof is a funny thing, we see what everyone else is doing, and feel stupid if we are not doing the same thing. And for me, even though I hated the idea of school and having to go back, I knew I had to at least try it at some point. The only way I would know for sure whether it was for me or not was by giving school a solid shot. I was always curious as to what I could do if I really set my mind towards pursuing secondary education. School was always on the back burner for me, making a real attempt at it seemed to be the only way I would put my mind at ease. I had avoided the topic for so long, it was time to finally face my fears, and expand my horizons.

I really wished the answer was clearer for me; that someone could knock on my door, and hand me a card with the answers saying "this is your future, have a nice day". I wanted so badly to just be able to figure everything out, and at the same time was torn between my dream of becoming a touring musician, and a working stiff. Conforming wasn't the answer, I never enjoyed working for other people. Being a musician had so much freedom, creativity, and leisure time. How could I pass up such an easy life style by going to school for something I didn't enjoy? I never would answer my door to a magic note full of life answers, I never had an easy time figuring things out for myself, and I wasn't supposed to.

Wishing for things to change and not doing anything to fix it is like being thirsty and complaining to an empty glass. You will never get the results you're looking for and will usually waste a lot of valuable time in the process. In order to truly get over your fears, you must face them head on. It may be a struggle, but at least you will know for sure whether you made the right decision at the end of the day or not. We as humans love to cower away from anything that gives us pain, anything that changes our schedules, and life in any way. Change is a great thing, it allows us to grow, to experience, to be challenged more than we usually would be. Even though school was frightening to me, I wanted to see what I was capable of, and the only way I was going to get this monkey off my back, was to step foot into a new role in my life.

I wanted so badly to become something more, and no matter how hard I tried, my music life wasn't happening the way I wanted it to. I wasn't touring full time, I wasn't playing sold out shows to hundreds of people every day, I wasn't doing anything I wanted. So with a big gulp of my ego, I decided to make the leap into post-secondary education. I had no idea what I wanted to do, but I knew that if I didn't at least try, I would never truly realize what I was missing. It was time for me to start becoming an adult, whether I wanted to or not.

CHAPTER 4

The belief

There comes a time in everyone's life where they reach some type of breaking point, or some type of realization of their own abilities and talents. They come to a point where they realize who they are, why they're the person they are and what direction to take. When I started my first attempt at post-secondary education, I realized why I was so resistant to the idea of school; I had closed my mind off to my own capabilities.

Now, let me be very clear when I say, university or college is not a bad thing to go through. For a lot of people, they cannot get to where they want to be in their careers without some sort of education behind them. Not everyone is made for school, and I was definitely one of those people. I never enjoyed the first days, the awkward finding your way through the unknown hallways, trying to find your first class, meeting all your teachers for the first time, feeling completely unorganized and lost, not knowing anyone around you, having to make new friends. I had no clue what I was doing, and I was nervous as hell doing it.

It dawned on me that a lot of kids my age were all going through the same things, and people much older than me were in the same boat as well. I decided I wanted to go for a criminal justice degree and become a police officer. I've never been a law breaker, and thought the idea of being in law enforcement was pretty exciting. I had to come up with the idea on my own, and it took a lot longer than I wanted.

I decided to step up and take on university for the first time, and was nervous for my first class, criminal justice. My class had a few people 20 years older than me pursuing higher education, which scared the crap out of me. While growing up, you think that most, if not all adults have their lives together. You think of them as well put together people who are set in their ways, working at the same job for many years before reaching retirement and relaxing at their cabins for the rest of their days. But I came to realize that this is not the case for quite a lot of older people. And it made me start to wonder about my own life, and what exactly I was trying to pursue.

It's a pretty disheartening thing to listen to 40 something's talk about how they spent their years in university for a degree they ended up hating, working at a job that bored them to death, only to end up right back in school again. My eyes widened as I listened to these people talk about the thousands of dollars they spent trying to further their education, only to wind up tremendously disappointed with the outcome. I was already starting to share that same emotion.

My criminal justice class was my favorite class by far. It was taught by an older woman who had the personality of an overly excited young kid; not in an immature way, just in a very passionate, happy way. She was truly a wonderful teacher to learn from. It was unfortunate to see her leave a few months into school due to health issues. Her replacements never did a good job at replacing her energy for the subject, and the class, became boring like all the others. One thing that really bugged me was taking classes that had nothing to do with what I wanted to get a degree for. I didn't see the point of paying for a 3 hour English course on ancient poetry that I was required to take in order to get my credit hours. Have you ever seen an episode of cops where an officer arrested a criminal while using sonnets from Shakespeare? Me neither. Either way, it took me about a month and a half of taking this course before I decided to drop it.

University was becoming more and more of a gong show in my eyes than something worth pursuing. My psychology class was usually filled to the brim with over 100 students, watching our professor sit at his desk while he read the slides on the projector. I was spending good money to have someone teach me something I could have read myself at home. Eventually I began not showing up for class every day and would make a mild effort at checking out the slides that were shown during class on our school's student website. I was becoming very disheartened with my choice to pursue a secondary education. I had spent a good chunk of my savings on something I wasn't learning much from. The experience turned into a chip on my shoulder, as I started thinking negatively of school once again. Instead of looking for an opportunity, I was looking for anything negative I could see in the situation. Not a good habit to get into in life.

University was not going to be my future by any means, and I did not have the money to waste on attempting something I didn't enjoy. I started coming to terms with what I had begun seeing in my life. The following year I decided not to go back to school and instead went back to work. My confidence in myself had been shot at this point. I had pushed through so much fear to go back to school, only to realize that it was not for me. Now I was really worried, but things were starting to look up in my musical life.

Around the beginning of my only year of university, my band started getting offers to play some bigger shows with touring bands coming into the city. These were huge opportunities to showcase our songs to kids who wouldn't ever see us during normal local shows. We played for a few bands I had grown up listening to, and even a few I didn't like, but who had a huge following. Most of the shows sold out, and we were lucky enough to be a part of the party. I remember having to leave class early one day so I could make it to the venue down the street for soundcheck.

This was a mind-blowing, exciting time in my life. School was not panning out the way I wanted, but my dreams of becoming a big time touring musician were becoming more real every day. My band started doing some really cool things that I never dreamed we would ever do. We began writing a full album, shooting music videos, and getting on bigger and bigger shows. Even though we were doing everything on a pretty small scale, I felt like a rock star in the making. One of the coolest experiences was releasing our first ever music video. I never dreamed it would happen, but seeing my band on a well shot video, while we sang our own song, was truly a mind-blowing thing for me. The music video brought the band some much needed attention, a lot more than I had expected. We were able to get on bigger shows, so big in fact, that we were asked to play a huge fundraiser at the largest venue in our city, the MTS centre.

Getting that phone call feels like it was yesterday. Our bassist had submitted our music to a local charity that was putting on a huge concert for young kids from many different schools across the city. It was a drug awareness event, and something I was really stoked to be a part of. When I was told we had been chosen to play at the MTS centre, I instantly got chills down my back. Even writing it gives me that same feeling to this day. I wanted a lot of things to happen with my musical life, but I had no idea music would bring me to the biggest stage our city had to offer. Dumbstruck, I could not contain my excitement. Playing an arena at the age of 20! Life is one heck of a ride.

The fundraiser was quite the crazy day. We had to be up for 4 am, to be at the venue for 6 to load in all of our gear. This was the day I really saw my passion for music at an all-time high. Being so eager to get up that morning, I don't think I slept more than a few hours. The alarm went off and I instantly shot up out of bed and was ready to go. The day went by in a flash; we loaded in our gear, and set up our merch table. Then we were brought backstage to our own personal dressing room, and spent the day hanging out with friends before going on stage. I have never been more nervous for a show in my life. Balancing out my excitement, I was worried about how my voice was going to hold up, or how our band was going to do.

A lung infection had kept me up for quite a few nights prior to the show, literally worried sick that I would not be able to play. I was just healthy enough to get enough of a voice to push through the show.

Soon it was our time to go up on stage. The whole set came and went in what seemed like only a few seconds. The crowd seemed mildly entertained by the music, and even more so by my speech at the end of the set.

Every singer from each band was asked to make a speech on why they chose a life of sobriety, and I had come up with what I thought was a pretty solid speech. But of course, what I had written on paper did not come out even close to what I said on stage. I don't remember the speech, but I do remember looking out at the sea of people and realizing how thankful I was for the opportunity I was given. There is nothing more exciting in my opinion than seeing the reaction a crowd has to your performance; no drug can ever top such a thing.

We finished the set, and I thought we played decently. The crowd response was mildly interested, and the claps at the end of the set were just loud enough to be polite. I thought they hated us. We were the only band at that show playing our style of heavy metal. My voice was rough due to my cold, but it was also the singing I did for our style of music. I couldn't tell whether kids were really into us because they genuinely enjoyed our set, or because we were just the entertainment at that moment in time. Either way, when I got off the stage, I was bummed out.

Walking up the stairs towards the main floor to our merch table where two of my friends were sitting, I dropped off my backpack and told one of my friends I was going to the bathroom. When I turned around, a line of kids had begun to form behind me, with the first one in line holding a piece of paper for me to sign.

There are not enough words to truly express how humbling the next two hours of that day were for me. More and more kids lined up to take pictures, ask for autographs, and share a story about why our performance touched them. It turned out there were a lot of heavy music listeners in the crowd, a lot of them were bummed they couldn't crowd surf or push mosh for us due to security. I signed everything from phones, belts, shoes, even foreheads that day. Kids were willing to literally ruin their clothes and expensive gadgets, just to have my name scribbled on them. Unbelievable experience and one I will never forget. It was the day I realized I was made for something bigger and better in my life. I didn't necessarily know what it was yet, all I knew was that I had a passion for people. When that happens, you're not going to stop pushing that passion, no matter how hard it gets along the way.

This day brought a sense of hope inside of me, that my dream was not dead. It gave me a real driving purpose to keep going forward with what I wanted to do with my life. It gave me clarity on my vision and allowed me to see my impact on even a few kids. It proved to me that I had chosen the right path for my life. That listening to the naysayers in life will not get you anywhere, and that we are responsible for what we accomplish. I did not know what the future held for me with music, but I knew that my future was never going to be the same after this day. And my drive was stronger than ever to create a life of purpose for myself.

This day allowed me to reflect on my early days as a drummer; a kid who loved the instrument but wasn't particularly talented at it. While also remembering the mocking, the words of criticism that were constantly thrown my way, only to be heard by deaf ears. The years I spent in the local music scene being mocked and talked down to by kids that didn't like our music and every person who never believed in us. The many shows to empty venues in sketchy neighborhoods, all added up to an amazing opportunity.

When I was first given the opportunity to become a singer, I had absolutely no idea what I was doing. I had always dreamed of being the guy on stage screaming his heart out and having kids look up to him in awe. I wanted to be the person making the most impact. A lot of times what happens is, when people are faced with an opportunity they are not ready for, they decline it. They say things like "it's not the right time" and end up squashing their dreams before even giving themselves a chance to see how it goes. Sometimes it's just about taking a risk, and working your butt off to learn along the way.

When I first started singing, I could barely go one song without my throat killing me, and having no more air in my lungs. I sucked hard, but I loved every minute of it, and knew I would get better over time. I never thought to myself "maybe this isn't for me" because I was going to make it be for me. Through strong faith and belief in myself I knew my vision was going to work out; that I was not going to allow any sort of road blocks stand in my way.

Too many people lack the belief within themselves to accomplish things they want in life. They say no towards their dreams before they even try. You must have an unwavering faith that somehow, some way, things are going to work themselves out. You have to work your butt off, push through the tough days, study whatever you need to study to become better, and always keep progressing forward. Faith backed by consistent work and action will make it happen. Sometimes you have to jump into things you may not be ready for, and learn along the way. If I never said yes to the opportunity to become a singer, I would have missed the opportunity of a lifetime. The opportunity that changed me, and shaped my future to what it is today, absolutely amazing.

You have to believe in your dreams so hard that you cannot be stopped by anyone or anything that may stand in your way. You must rely on your passion and dedication to your craft, to get you through the hard times. Come to the understanding that everything you want takes time, it will not happen overnight. It took me nine years to play in an arena, and many, many shows where no one even showed up. Consistent and persistent action taking will allow you to achieve whatever it is you are going after. If I were to have quit at any point before this day, people would have told me it was a good idea. And I would never have seen what my life was truly capable of becoming. How sad would that have been? This book would not exist if I were to have given up at every hard turn and roadblock I was up against. You have to be willing to sacrifice your time, your freedom, your everything, if you want something bad enough in life. I may not have been a Rockstar by any means, but damn did I feel like one that day.

Chapter 5

Decluttering

Success in life is as difficult to understand as it is to achieve. In order to find true success, whether it be in business, friendships, relationships, or anything else, we cannot be surrounded by negativity. This is as true for the people we spend our time with, as it is for the places we spend the most time in. Negative people with negative view points on themselves and their lives only seek to destroy the good in us. When you're a dreamer, an optimist, or a goal oriented person, negativity will always find you. The trick is to not let it touch you for very long, to not let the negativity affect your actions or your thinking. And realizing, if you do allow negativity to come into your life, you are allowing for success to be pushed further and further away.

When I began down the road of my personal development and growth as a person, I was met with a lot of harsh criticism. The great part about changing your life and your circumstances in more positive ways is, you see firsthand who your real friends are. Those people who will stand by you, during both the most difficult times, and the most successful times of your life. The people who stand up for you and who build you up, not kick you while you're down like everyone else. It's one of the most difficult life lessons we must face if we want to gain more value in our lives. We will lose friendships along the way; not everyone that started the journey with us will be at the finish line.

When I began changing the style to which I wrote my music, I started noticing a pattern of disconnect from a lot of people. Many of the musicians I was surrounded by spoke about very angry topics, or didn't care too much about what they wrote at all. I found myself connecting more with bands that spoke a message of hope, prosperity, and positivity. I remember traveling to the states one summer for a heavy music festival full of bands playing the same style music as my band. One in particular truly blew me away. Their name was Stick to Your Guns, and their vocalist was by far one of the most passionate speakers I had ever witnessed in person. He spoke with so much power and was truly confident in his ability to change people's mindset towards life, and humanity's most difficult situations. He spoke about politics, human rights, and many other things that got people thinking. It brought a whole new vibe towards the music they played, and I resonated with it in a very big way.

I wanted to start writing my own positive message within my own music. Being the vocalist of my band was one of the most important responsibilities, and one that I loved so much. As the face of the band, the voice people heard between songs, I was the guy whose words you listened to in our music. I felt it was my responsibility to bring real value into the lyrics I had written in our songs. Writing lyrics was like therapy for me, I was able to let out a lot of pent up resentment and anger that had been stored away during my teenage years. Many of the songs I wrote lyrics to have references to stories I share in this book, it was my way of putting the final cherry on top of the difficult years growing up. I even started posting more positive messages on social media, which is where I began to receive some unwanted negative opinions.

The whole spreading hate thing on social media is something I never really understood. Especially towards someone the person follows. When I started posting more positive stuff on my social media pages, I began receiving messages from people telling me to "stop acting like some rock star hero" and "nobody cares" when referencing the subjects I was talking about. I have to say, a lot of this negativity affected me deeply, and hurt me, as it had come from old friends who I was once close to. I couldn't understand why people could not see the good in what I was trying to do.

The posts were not meant to shove down people's throats; I was sharing my story on how I was able to play an arena at the age of 20. The idea of it seemed so crazy and unbelievable to me, that I wanted to share my "if I can do it, you can too" story. Some people saw it in the way I intended, others did not. It was something I was going to have to get used to. Because in order for me to become the person I was going to be, I needed to start trimming the fat. It was time to start letting go of a lot of people. It was the only way I was going to become happier, but to do this took a lot of work. It's not easy cutting out people you were once close with, but I knew there was no way around it; my old life was not doing me any favors.

I'm a very social person, always have been, and always will be. I can be shy and reclusive like anyone else, but deep down, I love spending time with people. As a kid, I tried very hard to make friends and have lasting, meaningful relationships with people. A lot of people can share stories about summer days spent with their best friends goofing off, hanging out every day, and going on crazy adventures. I never had that, I don't know why, but I always seemed to find myself around people who disrespected me. People who enjoyed hurting me, and somehow, I would never do a thing about it.

One summer, I really wanted to spend time with a good friend of mine from school. I was in junior high at this time, and had known quite a few kids for the majority of my life. I always had a lot of fun with one particular kid who I'd gone to school with since kindergarten. We played on soccer teams together, as well as hung out at school, I always thought of him as a great friend. He lived close to my house, only a few minutes on bike from my front step to his. That summer I started hanging out with him, and was having a great time doing it. I would ride my bike over every day, and knock on his door to ask him to come hangout. We would play soccer, basketball, tennis, ride our bikes. I was having a lot of fun and thought it was the best summer I'd had in a long time.

Unfortunately for me, my friend did not seem to find the hangouts as fun for very long. The more I wanted to hangout, the less interested he became in wanting to spend time with me. Maybe I annoyed him with my every day stops by his house, maybe I was boring to him; who knows. I never thought I was annoying, it was never my intention. I just wanted a good friend to spend time with. Eventually, he began avoiding me, even getting his younger brother to lie about him not being home, while hiding in a back room of his house. It probably took me a little longer than I would like to admit to realize I had to stop asking him to hangout. I never went out of my way to spend time with him like that again. The day his little brother had to cover for him was the straw that broke the camel's back. It hurt me deeply to see someone get sick of me, when all I ever wanted was to be his friend.

It's funny how we fight for people to stay in our lives when we shouldn't. We hold on as tight as we can when these people want nothing to do with us. I hated being alone at a young age, but I knew in order to be better for myself and my future, I had to start learning how to accept it. I began cutting people out of my life slowly but surely. It started with not coming to hangouts, avoiding any offers for coffee; doing anything and everything possible to start cutting out the negativity in my life. I was beginning to see more and more who my true friends were, and it was pretty crappy to see just how small that list of people was. It's not about how many friends you have; it's about the amount of value that select few people bring into your life.

Around this time, I even started changing my surroundings, spending more time working on my physical health by going for walks, and exercising in my home gym. Through pushing my body to become healthier, I found relief and therapy and I loved being outdoors and exploring new neighborhoods. My standards for my own life were beginning to change drastically. I began seeing less hate towards me, because I stopped paying attention to it. Out of sight, out of mind, you can't feel the burn if you're nowhere near the fire. My personal value was changing, and I was starting to see more beautiful people come into my life. It's so crazy to see the power of a positive mental attitude towards life and how it can completely change the world around you. I realized how much time I had wasted feeling sorry for myself and letting others take me down a negative path filled with teenage angst and over the top emotions.

The trick to life is to prevent yourself from being misguided by other people. We should never allow our lives to be dictated by what others think, say, or do. In order to change our lives we must first change our mindset towards life as well as towards ourselves. We cannot place our happiness into places, people, or things. True happiness is not a destination you get to, and stay in. It's through the process of accomplishment, through working on yourself and something that you are passionate about. Happiness is not a destination; it is a journey, a process we must all go through. But in order to go through it, we must make the necessary changes within our environment and our minds.

We must allow ourselves to let go of the past, and move forward into the future with a clear mind, and a happy heart. To know the feeling of true freedom, we must first disconnect from all negative ties that are holding us in place. Too many of us are chained down by our past, letting it drag us down deeper and deeper into a hole of resentment, and self-pity. We must remove the chip from our shoulders, learn to forgive our past, and not look back on it with a driving emotion. Instead, we must use our past as a learning tool, to drive us down the road we want to go down in life. That's where success is found, looking forward and dreaming bigger. If you cannot change something that has already happened, let it go, its unnecessary weight not worth carrying.

CHAPTER 6

Living life for yourself

The momentum had started building after my band's show at the arena. I was buzzing off the vibes I had received from so many kids for days afterwards. We had a CD release coming up in a few short weeks, and I knew that fundraiser would help us a lot with our ticket sales. It was a big release for us. We had put together 7 of our best written songs over the course of 2-ish years, and could not wait to get the music out to everyone. Planning a CD release can be a lot of work, but the results can pay off quite well if you do it properly. We asked a few of our friend's bands to open the show for us, the venue we were playing was one of my favorites in the city; it all came together quite well.

I saw a glimpse into a new skill and passion that I didn't really know I had until the big fundraiser show. Connecting with people, speaking on stage and sharing my story was what I loved and flourished at. The impact it made on so many kids that day made me realize I had something I needed to work on in a big way. My entire perspective as a vocalist and musician changed that day, and I started seeing the responsibility of choosing my words and the way I presented them properly. I had uncovered what I really enjoyed doing in life the most. It wasn't so much the music, but the passion for connecting people that drove me to do it. My strength was building people up through my stories, and the music was a great way to do it.

The CD release day came, and I was beyond excited. All of our friends and family were planning to come out and watch us play. We had worked our butts off at selling as many tickets as we could. Our drummer was particularly talented at leveraging his friendships with so many people, into ticket sales. He was a great salesman and helped us tremendously in our success of that show. I showed up to the venue with so much enthusiasm and excitement. I knew we had sold a good chunk of tickets, but I was just excited to finally showcase these new songs we had been sitting on for well over a year. After setting up the merch table, I did my sound check, and started greeting friends as they came in. The buzz about our arena show helped us quite a lot. People looked at us like we had just finished a tour with Metallica, they were so excited for us, and so excited to see us, it felt so great to finally see the hard work paying off.

The opening act got on stage and started the show off with a bang, they were the perfect band to open for us. Super heavy and energetic, got the crowd going right away. The room was already half full during the first bands set, I was so excited by that. "Even with this many people, this show can be amazing" I thought to myself. I walked around the venue and greeted friends and family who had begun to show up. Congratulating us and excited to hear us play. You could feel the energy in the room building to a massive scale, a moment that has never been lost on me.

I never get nervous for shows in a bad way, some people take the pressure of going up on stage in front of people as a bad thing. A lot of people experience stage fright, which to me I could never understand. I loved every second I was on stage. It was scary yes, but in the best way ever. Whenever we were about to play a big show with lots of people in the crowd, I would always get the same question from someone, "are you nervous?" Hell yeah, I was nervous! Not because I'm afraid of being judged or people mocking us on stage, that will always happen. I was more nervous about my own voice, making sure I sounded great, and didn't mess up any lyrics. The ability to go up on stage and perform for people was a blessing to me. The more people in the room, the more people I got to showcase my talent to. The more people that were willing to stick around and listen to us play, the better shows were. The more people that actually took an interest in what we did, gave me more of an opportunity to inspire someone.

If I could inspire, or help change someone's views on life in any way shape or form, I would be satisfied. I wasn't looking to change the world, I would be happy if even one person took my music's message to heart. All I wanted was the chance to be the person I always wanted to be, even if it was for as little as an hour. Being on stage allowed me to have an outlet I could not find anywhere else. It allowed me to express myself in a powerfully emotional way, and gave me the chance to let out a lot of pent up emotion. I always wanted to be up on stage in front of big crowds, singing along to my words and giving me as much energy as I gave them. Thankfully, I got to live my dream by becoming a singer.

Going backstage during the last few bands sets, I loved not watching the show for a while. Then checking back in a bit later and seeing how many more people had shown up. I also needed a break from talking to so many people, my voice would lose its power before I even hit the stage at the rate I was talking to people. My pre-show ritual was to stay in a back room, listen to some music, practice my vocals and warm up my voice a bit; while mentally preparing for the show.

When I walked back out to check on the show, I couldn't believe how many people there were in the room. The floor was packed, kids were going crazy, and best of all, we hadn't even stepped on stage yet. I was so stoked to have all my friends playing the show, getting a chance to play in front of a crazy crowd and have them enjoy the show as much as we did. To this day, many of the guys in those bands have told me that our CD release was the best show they have ever been a part of. I watched in awe from the side of the stage as the last band before us finished their set. The room had gotten even more hectic since I had last checked in on it. Now I was really nervous, in an overly excited kind of way.

My band mates came backstage to get their stuff together for our set. You could see it in all our eyes, we were stoked. So many years of hard work paying off in one moment, it was the best feeling in the world.

At the time, a friend of mine was putting together a photo project where she would ask people, "What advice would you give to your younger self?" It was a pretty easy question for me, and I wanted to have the picture taken during my bands set. She put my quote on a large white piece of paper, so I could hold it up half way through our set, in front of the crowd. To this day, I still have the photo on my bedroom wall, as a reminder of what hard work and dedication to something you love looks like.

Finally, it was our time to get on stage, the butterflies in my stomach were going crazy. Even though we were the headliner, and the show was for us, I still had a worry in the back of my mind that people would leave before we started playing. You never wanted to be the headliner of a show that went too late, if people don't care about your band, they will leave in very large groups. I don't even want to talk about the number of great crowds we missed out on because we were last on the bill. We set everything up, I did a few checks into the microphone, and with a few thumbs up, the sound guy was ready for us to start our set.

The lights dimmed, the crowd got louder, and my band mates and I huddled together for our pre-show ritual. A little pep talk, high fives, and we were ready to kick some serious ass. I can still see the crowd like it was yesterday, our first song came in with a loud bang, and the lights lit up the room. All I could see was a mass of bodies, literally moving together like a wave in the ocean. I have never seen a crowd go so wild for us. Kids were pushing each other, punching and kicking everything, and stage diving like crazy. The energy in the room was so intense, it made the set that much better.

About half way through our set, I brought out the card with my advice to my younger self written on it. "Don't let people change who you want to be or where you want to go" were written in big black letters. I showed the crowd my card, and spoke on my experiences in music, and how I struggled dealing with a lack of support from kids around me, and how people had told me to stop following my dream. That show, was one of the pinnacle moments in my life, it truly started defining who I wanted to become as a person and the legacy I wanted to leave behind. A positive influence to young kids, a better example of what you can be in your life if you hold on to what it is you want to do more than anything else. And never allowing the words of others dictate the direction you want to go in life.

We never get to see what we are capable of in life until we push aside the fear of failure and embarrassment, and move forward with passion. Far too many people live their lives in fear of judgment and worry, constantly feeling dissatisfied and not having a clue as to how they can change it. We all deal with judgment and ridicule at some point in our lives, we all have to start at the bottom at some point. The whole purpose of going through the beginning stages is to learn, strengthening our own abilities, and pushing through the hard days.

Living a life that we want is never going to be easy, but nothing worth having in life is ever easy. We must be in tune with our own abilities, our own skill sets, and our own passions, and move forward with them. We all have something we love doing, we all have something we dream about becoming, the only thing that stops us from living out those dreams is our own minds. Our minds are telling us what we can and cannot do because we are so used to hearing it from the outside world. Shut out the noise, listen to your gut, and follow whatever path makes you the happiest. Don't worry about those who belittle what you do, no matter what path you take in life, they will be there to judge and hurt you. You might as well do what you want to do anyways, and be happy, instead of living your life for other people.

CHAPTER 7

Patience is key

Patience is a skill that takes a lot of effort to achieve. I have never been one for being calm, cool, and collected when it comes to my own life. I used to get so impatient, so frustrated, so uncomfortable, if things were not going the way I wanted them to go. You ever had that voice inside your head that keeps bugging you, and no matter what you do to ignore it, it just pesters you until you explode? I have had this more than once in my life.

After my band's CD release, things began slowing down a bit with the band. We were never the band that could keep the momentum going, it was a constant roller coaster of teasing people who were interested in what we were doing. We would catch the attention of a bunch of people, and then stop doing things due to everyone's busy schedules, we would continue this cycle over and over again. It was not our intention what so ever, life got in the way more than a couple of times. You can't expect everything to go perfect with a group of guys who are all trying to grow up and figure their lives out. It was frustrating for me because I was setting aside most of my life to continue pushing this band forward. My band mates all were pursuing their careers in school or full time work, and I was the only one holding onto a retail job just to free up my time, and dedicate everything towards music. Or at least that's what I told myself for a long time. Laziness may have also played a factor, along with not wanting to waste time in school all over again. I was fearful of getting back into growing up, and did not want to be disappointed in the end results. Fear drove me to waste more time than I should have, but at the time, all I wanted was to tour and be stoked on life.

I was finding it hard to motivate the guys in my band, and I was starting to lose a lot of hope in what I had spent so much of my life being dedicated to. My parents always told me to never throw all of my eggs into one basket, and that working with people who are not all in will lead to hardships along the way. And I was finding that out faster than I wanted to. I started becoming very hard on myself and felt as though I had just wasted the last many years of my life on something that did not return to me what I had put in. Anger built up within myself for not seeing the forest through the trees. I had put my entire life on hold in order to play music, and no matter how hard I tried, I could not make it work out the way I had hoped. It wasn't my bandmates fault, they were doing what they needed to do to survive. I was just too stubborn and fear driven to actually do something more outside of music. I created my entire life and personality around my music, and it left many other aspects very empty.

I don't know how, but I convinced my band to go on tour one more time. We had done a two-week western Canada run with some friends of ours from Ontario, a few years earlier, and it was one of the best times of my life. This time, we made the tour even longer, with more dates, more days off, and no other band joining us. Going on tour with another band was always so fun, but it made it harder to book shows when the promoters had no idea who either of the bands were. They did not want to risk their own money to pay two bands, and have the show not do very well. Whenever a band came through Winnipeg, our guitarist and drummer would have them stay at their place for the night. They would feed them, offer them a warm place to stay, and even let them do laundry. That was just who they were, very kind dudes who wanted to look out for bands strictly out of the goodness of their heart. They never did it for bragging rights or to get anything out of it. So, when it was our turn to go out on the road, we had a lot of people willing to take us in and help us out.

The heavy music scene in Canada can be pretty tight knit, and if you have a solid reputation for supporting local bands and helping them out like we did, you were treated well for it. We tried as best as we could to always show up to shows for the bands that toured to Winnipeg. We knew what it was like coming to a new city and having no one come out to your show. We booked all the dates ourselves, finding contacts however we could, either through messaging other bands or searching event pages on Facebook and finding the promoter through there. We were able to secure a solid two and a half weeks of dates from Manitoba, to British Columbia, and back. Some of the shows were larger cities, others were small towns in the middle of nowhere. We found that the smaller towns made for some of the best shows, because kids there were a lot less spoiled with concerts happening in their town, so they took advantage of every opportunity that they could.

This tour was a highlight of my life for sure, as I got to live out my dream life for a few weeks. It was a vacation, but instead of relaxing on a beach, we were playing shows. I got to travel the country with my best friends, and explore places I never even knew existed. I never really cared if we had a ton of kids come out and support us, although it would have been greatly welcomed. I just wanted to have a few people there to play to and have fun with. Especially since some drives took 12-16 hours, I wanted those trips to be worth it. At the end of the day, I was just thankful for the opportunity to travel the country and play music at all.

Throughout this entire tour, I knew that this would probably be the last time my band ever had this opportunity again. It was a scary thought, but I knew I was being realistic. Every member of the band was working a construction trade, and a few were working out of town quite often, which made getting together for practices that much more difficult. I was the only one who had not started working, what I considered, an adult job, and was still clinging onto the dream of becoming a touring musician. It was a hard pill to swallow, but I didn't want to think about it too much while the tour was going on. I just wanted to enjoy every moment I could while I still had the chance to.

Gratitude in life is very important; you have to learn to appreciate every blessing that comes your way. No matter how big or small, you have to live those moments to the fullest, because you have no idea if you will ever get to experience them again. We had more days off than on our last tour this time around, and it gave us the opportunity to explore the beautiful western side of Canada. From waterfalls, to clear blue lakes, to larger than life mountains, I witnessed some of the most beautiful pieces of Canada's wilderness. I even floated down the bow river in Calgary; a huge stretch of water that runs throughout the whole city. It was crystal clear water that had found its way from the mountains, I have never seen a river so clean and clear flowing through a large city like that. I was truly able to live life on that tour, and it was a chance I took to grow more as a person. I met so many friends, played so many amazing shows, and spent so many fun nights camped outside of Walmart in our band's van.

We soon made it all the way to Vancouver, playing a super sweaty show in a concrete garage in the middle of a sketchy neighborhood. That show was so sick, so many kids showed up into that tiny room and made us feel right at home as we played our hearts out. After the show, I was saying goodbye to some friends I'd made, when I realized something. Tomorrow, we were heading back where we came, making our way back home to play our last shows of the tour. A sudden sadness came over me as I started thinking about what I was coming home to, absolutely nothing. I had a job I hated, I had no girlfriend welcoming me back with open arms, and I was probably going to witness the demise of my own band. I of course always had my family to come home to, but there were some big chunks of my life missing, and I needed to change it quickly.

It was not something I was looking forward to at all. My band mates had lives to come back to, jobs that they enjoyed, girls they couldn't wait to see, and I had nothing. The trip back home felt so much shorter than the trip out west, every show coming back went by as quick as it came. We made it to the border of Saskatchewan and Manitoba, and suddenly I was only a few hours from home. I remember seeing the Welcome to Winnipeg sign and feeling sick to my stomach.

We arrived at our drummer and guitarist's house, unpacked our personal belongings from the van, and went our separate ways. Our final show of the tour was in Winnipeg, we got back early enough that we could go back home, shower and change into clean clothes, see our families, and head to the show. I got home and was greeted by my mom at the door, she was very happy to see me after 3 weeks, and for a second I was happy to be home. After a few hugs and kisses, I walked into my room, threw my bags on the floor, and flopped onto my bed while a sadness over took my entire body. I had a bad feeling my band's life would never be the same after this tour. I had just spent every day for almost a month surrounded by my best friends, meeting new people, exploring the country, and living life the way I was always supposed to.

After taking a nap, I got ready for the final show, and had one glimmer of positivity in me; I wanted to take everything in one last time. I remember not wanting that show to end, and feeling so sad to go home. The next morning, I had to wake up for 6 am to go straight back to work. The dream came and went, and I was forced to go back to lame old reality.

The frustration and lack of patience really took hold of me after tour. I went back to my job, and hated every minute of it. So, I would go straight home after work and lie in bed watching Netflix until I eventually fell asleep. I spent my days worried and sick to my stomach, constantly over thinking about what I could be doing with the time I had. Instead of focusing on how I could make the very best of the time I had now, I was so concerned with how much time I had wasted. Worst yet, I was so impatient for changes to happen, I just wanted everything to be different overnight. I was so unrealistic with the way I was going about my life, and I was wasting valuable energy on my pity party. The way I thought about my life started to change when I began reading some valuable reading material. The first ever self-development book I read was *Think and Grow Rich* by Napoleon Hill. It was the first time I really started to look at my mindset towards life with a new perspective.

I have always been a bit of a negative person, not necessarily on purpose, just a talent I acquired through years of neglect and self-pity. So, when I decided to start developing more of a conscious mind towards what I was doing every day, I started seeing some serious bad habits that I needed to change. Patience was one thing I had to start changing; I was so focused on getting everything I wanted in as fast of time as I could, that I was not enjoying the process of getting to the destination I was shooting for. My anger towards my past was so strong that I had been letting it control my present for way too long. I would allow things that happened years ago to affect me in my everyday life, when I realized how much time I had wasted doing this, I immediately started working on changing it.

The idea of being patient is to allow for us to recognize that not everything we want in life is going to happen right away. Sometimes it's going to take days, weeks, months, or even years to achieve the things we want to accomplish in life. I began to see how giving up on music when I first started would have been detrimental if I had stopped at the first sign of struggle. We are not supposed to get everything we want whenever we want. The point of life is to work towards our goals and achieve as much as we can along the way, so that we can truly appreciate the results when they happen.

The process of finding peace of mind was a hard one to come to terms with. It took a lot of practice, a lot of forgiving, and a lot of reflection on my own mistakes. After some time, I began to realize that in order to become the best person I could be, I had to let go of every crappy emotion and vibe that had me shackled for so long. To cut those chains meant cutting the weight off that had held me down, and was not allowing me to grow as a person. We must grow every day and learn how to become better as people through giving more of ourselves to everything that we do. From putting our best foot forward at our jobs, to helping our family, and friends in whatever way they need. The way we become better is by bringing more value towards the world. By being patient through the process, and realizing that everything we want in our life is going to take time. But the process of growth is where true happiness is found.

CHAPTER 8

Learning along the way

I am a very hard working person. When I put my mind to something I want, I will do everything I can to achieve that goal. There is also a very lazy side to me as well, a side that says "I'll do that later" and then never does it. It is something that has not held up well over the years, as I have had to work harder for what I want more than ever. I have had to force myself into the mindset that if I want anything to get done, I have to be the one to do it. No one is going to take my hand and do the work for me. Anyone who wants success in life with anything that they do, needs to understand that in order to get what they want, they need to work. It doesn't necessarily mean back breaking work that can be quite physically demanding on your body. I have done many jobs that have put a huge strain on me physically, and they have been some of the hardest things I have ever done. Did I find the experience worth my time? Not necessarily. Was it an experience I needed to go through in order to understand that there are better ways for me to do things with my life and my work ethic? Of course it was.

I always thought that in order to work hard, you have to physically drain yourself for it to count. If you are not exhausted by the end of the day physically, you did not work hard enough. But as I got older, I realized that was simply not true. Hard work does not always have to be physical, it can come from doing something with so much passion and drive, that it does not feel like hard work. There are some people in this world that work tremendously hard at what they do, yet don't feel like they work hard at all. They are so in love with the process, that anything that they do for it is simply a blessing, something they can't wait to do.

Having been brought up in a very old school mindset kind of household, my parents have always been the very hard working, blue collar type of workers. My father came from a small town two hours outside of Winnipeg. He has always taught me the value of rolling up your sleeves and getting done what needs to be done, even if you don't want to. As a kid, my dad would get me to help him around the yard outside, raking leaves, or teaching me how to use the lawnmower. I even remember one summer having my dad teach me how to paint with a roller on our garage floor. He has always been the type of guy to step up and get the work done, no matter how crappy the job. He always tried to instill that work ethic into me. My mom grew up in the city, but came from a family of Italian immigrants, who knew what real hard work was all about. She was brought up in a family that took care of one another, and did not complain while doing so. Both my parents valued and respected hard work, so the second I was old enough to get a job, my parents were completely behind it.

Not many people enjoy working in their early teens. I wish I could have been born with that hard working gene at a young age like some people, but I wasn't. No matter what it was, school, soccer, work, I had a tendency to slack off until I would get a huge kick in the ass, and start doing really well. I was always capable of succeeding in everything I did, but my work ethic was a back and forth battle.

My mind was always elsewhere, and it was never around work. In school, I would get bad grades because of my lack of effort. Instead of putting time aside to study, which I found so boring, I would watch TV and lie that I had spent that time looking over my notes. It wasn't until parent teacher night when my parents had the opportunity to see for themselves the end result of this lack of effort. In the 7th grade, I was doing so poorly in school, my father had to threaten to take me out of soccer unless I did well. That scare tactic worked, because the next year I became an honor student, which proved to me just how capable I was if I put my mind to something and actually worked.

My first ever real job was a soccer referee at the age of 13. I had been playing soccer since I was very young, and my passion for it was immense. My mom thought it would be a really good idea to have me sign up to become a ref. "It will be good for you, and I'm sure once you get into it, you'll love it!" she encouraged me. The thought of refereeing soccer games never crossed my mind, but I thought "what the hell" and gave it a shot. I went through a few weeks of 3 hour classes after school, learning the ins and outs of a soccer referee and his duties. It was all old information for me, as I had played the sport long enough to understand everything the ref had to go through each game. What I didn't realize were the opportunities at hand for referees who were quite good at their jobs. Some would go on to help ref games in the FIFA world cup, which was huge in my eyes. After the long and boring night classes, I became certified. It didn't take me long before I began refereeing real games. It also did not take me long to realize there is a huge difference between playing a sport, and refereeing the sport. Many angry parents, players, and mistakes caused me to realize that it was not my calling. After the experience, I started realizing the value of working hard for your money. I was able to buy stuff for my drums, go to the movies with friends, little things that I could not do before. Even though I hated the work, I enjoyed the freedom it allowed me to have.

My next real job was working for a grocery store near my house at the age of 15. My mom was close with the wife of the store manager, and insisted I apply for a job there. There were no if ands or buts with my parents, once they decided it was time for me to get a job, that was it. I had no intention on working any job, all I wanted to do was play music and hang out with friends. Of course, I got the job quickly, and began working as a bagger for minimum wage. It was simple enough; bag customer's groceries, grab carts and garbage from outside, and hate your life while doing so. I never liked being told what to do, how to dress, when to go to the bathroom or when to eat. Always having a bit of a rebellion towards authority, in the mildest way possible, I was not one to pick fights with a police officer, or break the law. The freedom any teenager enjoys was what I was looking for, and was not ok with the shackles of working a job. I spent a few evenings and midday weekend shifts each week working for this store. It wasn't so bad at first, but eventually I began doing what every lazy kid who hates his job does. I found any excuse to go to the bathroom. My supervisors must have thought I had stomach issues, because I always ended up in there. It was usually just to sit down for a few minutes and catch a break. The constant moving around and standing for hours on end took a toll on my young self; such a hard life I led. Looking back on this job, and every job I had in the years to follow, it's actually laughable what I found as hard work. I spent 3 years at this job before eventually moving forward, landing a job at a shoe store with my best friend.

My best friend was the supervisor, so the job was easy. We spent most days fooling around in the back break room, making up silly games to pass the long boring night shifts. The job was ok, and taught me quite a lot about sales and how to approach potential customers. I had never tried selling anything in my life, but with this job I ended up finding some success. Eventually selling $4000 worth of shoes on more than one Saturday shift, one of the coolest few days I had at the job. I spent a year and a half with the company before moving on to a better paying job. It was at a milk shipping plant where I was able to find a job thanks to one of my cousins. The job paid way better than any of my previous retail jobs, the hours were steady and long, and I had benefits. All of these things did not matter to me in the slightest at the time. The drive to get to the warehouse was long, almost an hour each morning, and it was eating up my gas tremendously. I only spent a solid few months at the place before moving back to retail, although my parents were not happy with the decision what so ever.

The realization was that I did not like working physical labor jobs, as well as a job where I would speak to my fellow employee's maybe once or twice a day. A job that left you with way too much time to think and get down on yourself, it was not a healthy place for me. I was going through a rough time, and needed to be surrounded by happier people. I got a job at a hardware store, which I was over the moon about. The real reason I chose to go back to retail was simply out of laziness. The warehouse job did not allow for much freedom with my time. I was constantly doing heavy lifting and hard work I didn't enjoy. And when I found out the job would not allow me time off to play a big show with my band that was coming up, it was the final straw. Give a lazy person a job to do, and he will find the quickest and easiest way to get it done. It may not be done the best, but it will get done the fastest. I was a lazy person determined not to work a hard job I hated.

I spent 3 years at the hardware store, making many friends along the way. There I found some success in the midst of the job, getting promoted within my first month and a half. I also learned a harsh lesson about retail, not everything promised to you will be given to you, no matter how hard you work. The job was hard on my mental health. It gave me way too much time to think, and the lack of money, hours being constantly cut, and the lack of job fulfillment had taken its toll on me. I started realizing along the way that my value was not being met in this position. And soon it would be time to make big changes in my own life.

Every job I ever worked, was a stepping stone to teach me something. I learned many things about how to be a more a responsible human being, and by doing so, made major changes for myself in my own life. It was not something I planned on realizing, because I fought the idea of working hard for a very long time. Working hard is good, it is admirable, and it is what we need to do in order to progress forward in our lives. Nothing worth accomplishing in life will happen just by us wishing for it. Wishing and doing are two different things. In life, we must take action in order to get the results. When I am faced with a difficult situation, or work that seems too hard or lengthy, I have to focus on the end result. What am I doing this work for, remains my focus.

When someone works out, they are not putting the hard work in just because they want to feel pain; no one likes eating healthy foods all the time. The thing they are working so hard for, comes at the end of all the early mornings and late nights, the results. The feeling of satisfaction knowing that they accomplished something they worked so hard for. The realization of their capabilities is part of coming to the understanding that no one can get in the way of someone who has the will to fight for everything they want in life. Every job I worked, gave me an opportunity to grow, to see life in a different way. I met many people, I made a lot of mistakes, but also gained a lot of experience. I may have hated many parts of those jobs, but when I strip them all down the bare bones, they showed me where I wanted to go with my life. Those early years of working jobs I hated allowed me to grow as a person, and see the value in making money for yourself.

Far too many people I knew were wasting their time goofing off, and spending money on things they did not needed. I was fortunate enough to be pushed into the situations I was in, and I value it now more than ever. My life had more meaning than just a 9-5, working for someone else until I die. I don't condemn anyone for living that lifestyle, because I came from a family full of hard working 9-5 people, I just knew I was made for something more. If your heart is telling you to steer yourself in one direction, do not fight it. Do not allow others to dictate how you choose to live your life. I was told many times to do many different things with my time, and take many jobs I did not want to work. I chose what was right for me, and have been blessed with more opportunities because of that fact. In the words of my father, "Listen to everybody, make up your own mind", you'll thank yourself later.

CHAPTER 9

Stopping the chase

I have always been a negative self-talker, from a very early age my parents have told me I had the attitude of a pessimist. There was always something or someone to be mad at; I always held onto negative energy, and I would over think everything while taking much of the happiness in my life away. When over thinking and over analyzing my own life became a crippling activity I despised being a part of, I finally understood what I was doing wrong. Anyone out there who has high expectations for themselves will tell you how hard being an over thinker is. You constantly feel as though you are not doing enough for yourself right now, and in your future. You are constantly looking at people around you and comparing yourself to these people because you feel a deep resentment, and sadness for realizing someone is doing better than you in life. It is an awful habit, and one I had to learn to fix quickly within myself if I ever wanted to be truly happy with my own life.

The problem with me was, along with being an over thinker, I was a big dreamer. I was less of a "glass half full" type of person, more of a "what the hell is in the glass" kind of guy. I looked at the world with bright eyes, as well as realistic logic. Very weird and contradictory I know. I dreamt of bigger things for my life, but was also logical and negative in my thinking. "I will never be a big Rockstar, I come from Canada" or "I want to tour the world, but not many musicians get to do that with their lives". It was a silly way of looking at things, the problem wasn't helped by the people I was surrounded by. Anyone successful and happy in this world will tell you how important the people you surround yourself in life are. I had many roadblocks that I needed to face, and I was stubborn as a mule for thinking I could change them over night.

My music life came to an end with my band just as I had predicted. Coming home from tour was like putting a nail in the bands coffin. We did not practice together much after the tour had ended, and only played one more show before the end of 2014. No matter how many times I pleaded with the guys to do more with the band, they would not have it. Everyone's priorities had changed, and mine were slowly starting to do the same. I realized how empty I had made my life by only focusing on music. Yes, I had a lot of success with it, but I did not allow myself to grow in any other way, and felt stuck in a very one sided life. My job at the time was not making me happy, not one damn bit. I knew my potential far exceeded what I was doing with my life, and working that job was a prime example of wasting time in my comfort zone.

The 9-5 job, the corporate guy in a suit kind of job, the full-time work were things I always stayed away from. Instead keeping my life as open as I could to musical opportunities, and not letting anything stand in my way. The idea of giving up my time for a job I hated did not interest me in the slightest. I have always chosen places that gave me as much flexibility with hours and time away as I could. Money was of no concern, benefits, pension plans, anything that came with a full-time job had no effect on me. Music was my life, and I fought for it every step of the way.

For the first time in my life, my band was not a priority to me anymore. I began losing hope on doing anything big with my band again, and started looking at finding full-time work. Working retail taught me many things about myself: I do not like working weekends, I do not like working evenings, I do not enjoy working with students who always call in sick, I do not like working for minimum wage, and I did not like having my already low hours per week cut down to almost no hours per week. It might sound like whining, and it was, but anyone who has spent any time in retail will tell you, it's a frustrating place to be.

A good friend of mine and I went out for dinner one night. He worked for CN rail, and was doing quite well for himself. I began telling him about my band situation, how I needed to start looking at bigger and better options for jobs as I saw no future for myself with music at the moment. He started telling me to start applying to CN. Anyone who lives in Winnipeg knows someone who works for CN, they're a huge company, and are well known for paying people really well.

I took my friends advice and began applying for any job I could with the railroad. For the next 10 months, I applied to as many positions as I could. The waiting process between each job application was exhausting and stressful, sometimes taking up to 3-5 months to get a reply. What made things worse was waiting for so long, to then be denied every job posting. I held off on applying anywhere else because I really wanted a good paying job with this company, but as usual, the universe had a different plan. Any young person between the ages of 18-25 will tell you how frustrating it is trying to figure out your life, and find a solid job while doing so. Heck, most people could tell you how big of a struggle it is trying to figure out your own life, at any age.

At 21, I was broke, and had no idea what I wanted to do with my life. I had put off the idea of going after school, a better job, anything productive for so long. Now I was in a position where it was either now or never; find a well-paying job with full time hours, or go back to school for something. Neither one was something I wanted completely. If I had the choice, I would have been on tour instead. But I sucked it up, and pushed forward. After many months wasted on applying to the railroad, my next option was looking at the construction trades. From the time I was 18, my dad had wanted me to go to school for a trade. "It's great money, and you'll be able to use these skills forever" he'd tell me. He always used my many cousins and other family members who have done well for themselves by working construction as prime examples as to why I should listen to him. I bit the bullet, after many years of fighting my dad on the idea, I decided to start looking into the trades.

It was frustrating for me, I have never been a hands-on type of guy when it comes to work. I have never really been a work type of guy in general, and the whole idea of working construction seemed very boring and exhausting to me. Nevertheless, I began diving into every website I could find on construction trades in Canada, forcing myself to get interested in something I thought would benefit me well in the long run. My goal was to find a career, not a job. I wanted something I could be proud to brag about. When people asked me what I did for a living, and I told them "I work as a cashier at hardware store" I would see the look of embarrassment for me in their eyes. Nothing worse than having an old teacher or classmate come through your till, asking you how's life treating you, and you're looking at them ashamed like "Oh life's going really well for me, clearly". I have no disrespect towards people who work retail, don't get me wrong, it's a great place for students and people coming here from a different country to get work and experience while making a little money. The problem for me was, I had worn out my welcome. I was no longer ok with living a mediocre, passive existence.

My search for a construction trade was tough, I had no idea what I wanted to do as a career. Nothing really interested me so I stuck to the jobs that would pay the most. Electrician, elevator technician, plumber, whatever paid more than $30 an hour, I was down for. When I was 19 I had signed up for a plumbing course at Red River College, and was accepted soon after. I remember getting the acceptance letter in the mail and getting a sick feeling in the pit of my stomach. I knew that if I had shown my parents the letter they would make me go. I threw the letter away and never told my parents until years later. Letting the fear of doing bad in school, and giving up on my dreams, stop me from being educated. I always kicked myself for doing that, but at the time it wasn't what I wanted or needed. There were two different colleges in the city that offered construction trade programs, but due to the level of popularity the trades had gained in the recent years, the waiting lists were huge. Some programs had 2-3 year waiting lists just to be accepted, I knew if I had to wait that long that I wouldn't even want to take the course by the time it was offered to me. I started throwing my name into as many programs as I could. I told myself "as long as I can afford it, I will take the first thing I'm accepted into". It was like picking 5 different tickets for a lottery I didn't want to win.

Many months had gone by after the first few programs I had applied to, and had heard nothing from the schools. I continued to seek out different programs I could qualify for, and would throw my name in. While also continuing to look for work, I was hoping I could find an apprenticeship and avoid going back to school for as long as I could. It was very difficult to even have a face to face conversation with any employer. No one cared about how many years of retail I had worked, my volunteering hours through soccer, or my ability to "calculate prices with ease" that my mom suggested I put on my resume as a skill set. All they cared about was construction experience, and I had none. I would always hear stories of friends of mine who walked into a random construction company, threw down their resume, and were given a chance at an apprenticeship, or at least an entry level job that would lead to one. It was so frustrating trying to find anyone willing to give me a chance. The harder I pushed the idea of going back to school, getting a better job for myself and becoming more of an adult, the less it was happening. I was actually trying to change my life, and was still not achieving anything. What made it worse was the fact that I had to force myself to want this. I didn't want a full-time job, I didn't want to work construction, but I wanted money to become freer and to do what I wanted. In order to have more freedom, I was willing to put aside my happiness, or at least that's what I thought at the time.

At one point, I actually thought I had a shot at an apprenticeship. My mom brought an ad to my attention that she had seen in the local paper. It was a mechanical company looking to hire apprentices, I was so excited. I knew if it was in the newspaper that there was less of a chance people would see it, which meant the competition would be low. Running to my computer, I eagerly emailed my resume to the company. A few days later I was given a call while at work, asking if I would like to come down for an interview. I was so excited, and so nervous. "This is my shot" I said to myself, "no room for errors here". The shop was located in the sketchy side of the city. I had to park my car in front of what looked like a crack den. The interview went well, the gentleman I talked to had explained how he went from a laborer, to an apprentice, journeyman, foreman, manager, to the vice president of the whole company. I was impressed, and knew I could have the same story as him if given the opportunity. He asked me why I wanted the job, what my intentions were, any prior experience, and so on. I left the interview feeling fairly confident I had made a solid impression. He told me I would be hearing back from him in a week, so I waited. A week went by and no call, I started getting worried. Two weeks went by, still no call, now I was getting sick to my stomach. "My first and only shot at an apprenticeship, and I blew it" I said to myself, I felt so stupid. I replayed the interview over and over in my head, thinking about anything that could have possibly gone wrong in the process. I decided to follow up and give him a call. Turns out, they had already hired everyone that they needed for the position. So while I was waiting for 2 weeks to hear back on my shot at a future career, they had already made their decision a few days after seeing me. Leaving me hanging to worry myself to death and feel like a pile of crap. I hung up the phone pissed off, very unimpressed by the way they treated the situation. It would not be the last time I would deal with sketchiness within the construction industry.

One of my band mates recommended a renovation company to me, after hearing about my struggles with finding a job in the trades. The company was looking for a laborer, which meant it was entry level, and I actually had a shot at it. He gave me the name and address, and the next day I made my way down to the shop. I was greeted at the door by the owner, very nice man, tall with a deep friendly voice. I explained to him that I was recommended to his company by one of my friends. When he heard the name, the owner smiled and admired my friend for his work ethic and attitude. I was using the reference to push my name up whatever list there was of potential applicants. We seemed to hit it off quite well, I was really hoping I could get this job. He told me he would give me a call back by the next day, and he did. "We looked over your resume, and we would love to have you come aboard" my new boss said over the phone. I enthusiastically accepted the offer, and hung up. I had the biggest smile on my face, a grin you could have seen from space. With a loud "WOO!" I celebrated my new job, and was relieved to finally get away from the place I had felt stuck in for so long.

Now when I talk about this part of the story, I want to be perfectly clear when I say this. When you follow money as your solution to the problem you are trying to solve, you will NEVER get what you truly want or need. When your intentions are solely based on whether or not you are going to make a lot of money, you are lying to yourself if you think you will find some sort of happiness along the way.

It is a huge lie you will tell yourself because you are driven by the desire to have more freedom to buy whatever you want, do whatever you want, and brag about your new position in life. I spent far too many years chasing money, rather than focusing on what I was doing to create value within my own life. When I began telling people that I wanted to become a professional speaker, some would say "but man, you might have to start off by not getting paid", and my response would always be the same. The money will come, but what is important is taking any and every opportunity to do something that makes me happy.

To bring value into other people's lives, and to not waiver from the purpose I have within my heart to do something different was something that took me a long time to realize. My best advice for you, and something I wish I could have told myself back then would be: **Find the thing you cannot go a day without doing, something that makes you so happy, you cannot wait to get out of bed in the morning.** Money is important, and it can be used to do many great things for the world, and yourself. But do not be driven by it, do not let it consume you. Let the thought of becoming a better version of you, and striving to bring more value to the world around you, drive you. Money will come and go, but passion is what will last forever.

My search was over, my life saving job had arrived. I was finally in a position where I could really start to move forward with my life. "Finally" I thought, "I'm getting my life on track the way I wanted". But that was far from the truth, and I would have to learn that the hard way…

CHAPTER 10

The truth revealed

They never tell you how hard growing up is going to be. They never explain to you the difficulties of finding the right path, and realizing there are many you will go down before finding the right one. When I was growing up, finding a job I loved was hard. When I first started, I would enjoy the new experience, the honeymoon stage. But in a very short period of time, my mood changed. Suddenly the environment wasn't as happy, wasn't as interesting, and it bummed me out tremendously. Maybe I expected too much too quickly, maybe I was looking in all the wrong places, maybe my work ethic wasn't good enough. Either way I wasn't happy, and it only continued to get worse.

After working in retail for the first 7 or so years of my working life, I was ready for a big change. I began working at a renovation company, and soon learned my lack of skills did not favor me well on the job site. For the next many months, I worked as a laborer, I ripped apart kitchens and bathrooms. I lugged heavy appliances, I swept and cleaned, anything and everything that someone with my skill set was capable of. It was a bummer, I had expected to come in and start learning the tricks of the trade, but became the garbage boy. I soon realized that the only way I was going to be able to set myself up to be in a better position, was to go back to school and get certified, or so I thought.

After four months in my first construction job, I stepped away to go back to school. The many months of waiting for a trade school to get back to me was finally over. I was offered a five-month course on carpentry, it was something I wasn't super interested in, but decided to jump into as it was my first opportunity given to me. The next five months were a lot of fun, the best experience I have ever had in school. I made many friends, learned a ton about the carpentry trade, and was given a lot more confidence to go back into the working world, knowing I had something under my belt. I worked my butt off in school, finishing with one of the highest GPAs in my class, reaffirming my belief in hard work paying itself off and then some. During the early months of school, I began looking online for jobs. I knew that the day we graduated, I was going to be all on my own, finding a job among the rest of my classmates. I did not want to be in competition with anyone, so being prepared well in advance was my only choice. The day of my last exam, I got a phone call just as I had arrived at school. It was a concrete company who had been given my resume through another company I had applied to. They said they were interested in me coming aboard and was wondering how fast I could start. It was such a surprise, but one I was fully welcoming, as I had no idea if this opportunity would come again anytime soon. I accepted the job offer, aced my last exam, and off I was onto another job.

Heavy duty construction is a whole other ball game to what I was used to. The work was rough, the conditions were rough as it was mostly outside, and the guys on the crew were rough. I was a fish out of water on the very first day. I was hired by a company working on a very large project just outside the city. Showing up to the site the first day, and realizing how big the project was, made me nervous as hell. I had to go through quite a few hours of safety training before being let onto the site. Once finished, myself and a few others guys were picked up by one of the site supervisors, and dropped off with our crews. From the very beginning, I was doing the work no one else wanted to do. Rolling up left over tarps, picking up garbage, stacking wood, and being referred to as "boy" more often than not. That was my life day in and day out.

After working my butt off in school, to come to a job that I expected so much from and got so little out of, was incredibly disheartening. I never expected to be the foreman or anything close any time soon. But at least was hoping to be put into a situation where I could use my training and new knowledge to my advantage. That would never be the case, construction is a rough world, and you must prove yourself and your abilities every step of the way, educated or not. That's something they never tell you in school, you're probably not going to get a job you like right away. It felt like a boys' club, and I could never relate to the guys I worked with. They all had much different lifestyles than I did, and I felt like a weirdo anytime I spoke.

I spent 2 months with this company, before being laid off. I was hired on at the peak of winter, when they needed the most people. As soon as the weather was warmer, and the work slowed down, I was let go. As much as I was disappointed in losing my job, I was also relieved. I could not handle the miserable environment anymore. No one I worked with really seemed happy to be there. Every day my supervisor would express his hate towards the job with the crew. "Ugh, I'm @#$%ing miserable man" he'd say, expressing his opinion as though he knew what we were all thinking. I remember so many moments where I just stared out onto the site, realizing just how bummed out I was and saying to myself "this isn't forever, it's going to get better". Over and over again, I reminded myself that something was going to change, it had to. I visualized where I would rather be, the things I would rather be doing, my own little happy place. Anything that made the day go by faster, and perk me up was welcomed. Things were going to change, I was right, but it took a lot of work to get there.

It took me 6 weeks before I eventually found another construction job, I worked for many more months before eventually stepping away from the industry all together. It wasn't for me, the work was rough on me, the environment depressed me, and I could not see a future for myself in it. I realized that although I may have been educated, I was not experienced. And maybe it was bad luck, but I did not have the most pleasant experience within the industry.

The final straw came during my last job, a moment that could have cost me my life. I was working in a condo complex, where they had set up an elevator outside of the building. It was pretty sketchy to be honest, and not something I ever enjoyed riding on. But when you're doing the work I was, climbing 22 flights of stairs was pretty damn draining. One particular day, my coworker and I were standing at the front of the elevator, the operator had stopped to pick up two workers who were putting the finishing touches on the windows on one of the floors. They had two large rolls of metal brackets they were using to finish their work. They were wrapped together with tape, each piece stretching over 10 feet long and looked pretty heavy. The two workers seemed to be having a hard time holding onto the brackets, and decided to shove them into the elevator on an angle. I did not pay much attention to them, and continued talking to my friend. Suddenly, I felt a large force hit the top of my head, it was the metal brackets. They had slid from their position in the elevator and had landed on top of my head. Lucky for me, I was wearing my hard hat which absorbed much of the impact. If it had not been for my hard hat being on, the brackets would have slammed directly on my head, causing some serious damage, or breaking my neck. Everyone in the elevator looked at me with horror, asking if I was ok. I was lucky I didn't feel a thing, and pretended like everything was all good. It was a whole different story inside my head, as I was slowly freaking out while coming to terms with what had happened.

The construction industry and my career with it were just not going to work out. I had pushed the idea for a very long time because I wanted the money. As well, I wanted something new to experience, and I wanted something I could make a career out of. Everything sounds nice on paper, seeing big checks in your bank account is awesome, but when it's at the expense of your health, your safety, and your happiness, it's not worth it. I made the choice to step away from that world, and focus more on other things.

The point of all this was, I made an effort to get out of my comfort zone and try something new. I had let fear once again lead my life for so long, that I would never try anything new, causing me to constantly over think and wonder "what if". It took a lot of really rough days, many unsafe moments, to realize I was not where I wanted to be. I pushed myself to work harder than I ever have before. I went into environments that I was completely brand new to, and learned a ton in the process. I respect people who do that kind of work ten times more now, because I see how hard it is. It wasn't for me, and I was happy I realized it sooner rather than later.

We can fool ourselves into believing that something we think is right for us is what we should put our efforts towards. We convince ourselves and come up with excuses as to why something should work for us, solely because of one particular, more superficial thing. For me it was money, I wanted a lot of it, and was willing to force myself to enjoy something I really didn't. For others, it might be bragging rights, people want to have something cool to brag about, even if they hate themselves on the inside for it. I was dealing with far more behind the scenes at this point in my life, and I was in great need of big changes. Unlucky for me, my personal life was changing in more ways than I ever expected, but it brought me the most clarity I could have ever asked for.

CHAPTER 11

A day of loss

While you grow up, you get told a lot of things about yourself. Either good or bad, they connect with you. They change you, and sometimes can either make you look at the world in a positive or negative light. I have never been one to let go of things easily. I had a chip on my shoulder the size of a watermelon, and for so long I let it affect me. I always felt that I had something worth hearing, I have been through enough rough times in my life to really come to terms with how crappy life can be. But I have also seen how great it can be, which is why I knew I had to start spreading a better message.

It had been a few years since I posted my positive things online, and I even cut it out of my musical performances. I started feeling cynical towards the people who had told me my voice wasn't worthy of being heard. Everything changed for me the day my grandmother passed away.

One of the worst experiences anyone can ever go through is watching a loved one die. For my family, we had the awful experience of watching our loved one die for 3 months. My grandmother first began feeling ill around April of 2016. The previous few years, I saw my grandma go in and out of hospitals for many different reasons. Taking bad falls, surgeries, illnesses, etc. Almost every time she went into the hospital, we thought it was going to be the end. I remember sitting in the hospital the day before my 21st birthday, waiting to hear whether or not my grandma was going to pull through a really rough surgery. So when my grandma went back into the hospital in 2016, it was same old story to my family. It wasn't that my family did not care about the situation, because it was definitely a serious one that we all were deeply concerned about. It was unfortunate that we had become used to being in this situation with her.

My mom had informed me that my grandmother had contracted an infection. I found out later, that her kidneys were not functioning properly, and over the years had begun to deteriorate. My grandmother was an Italian immigrant to Canada, so her English was not the best. It would cause her more difficulties when speaking to doctors and nurses while in the hospital. Luckily my family was always there to help out every step of the way. Translating everything to get my grandmother the care she needed. She was brought into the hospital and treated for a few weeks, and was let out, but soon after was brought back in. It seemed like a constant struggle with my grandma. We would see glimpses of hope, and would immediately be brought back to reality.

I can still remember the last day I saw my grandma somewhat normal and healthy during this time. She had just been let out of the hospital, and my family and I decided to go visit her the next day. We walked into her room in her nursing home, and were greeted by her warm smile. I loved seeing the reaction on my grandma's face when I walked in the room. Her eyes would light up, she'd smile as big as she could, and give me a big hug and plenty of kisses. Even when she wasn't feeling her best, she always did her best for those she loved. There are very few people in this world who have ever treated me with as much love as that woman did. I told her how happy I was that she was looking so healthy and happy, her hearing was not the best at this time either, which did not help with the language barrier. Whenever my grandma spoke to one of us and didn't understand or hear what we said, she would smile, and laugh. That was the best reaction, she had the best smile, and the most infectious laugh. I remember the feeling I got while sitting in her room that day, something didn't feel right. I knew things had been very touch and go for her over the years, but this time it felt different. I spent the visit talking to her and holding her hand. We didn't need to talk about much, I just wanted to be with her. She always made me feel better, she always had love to give me.

Halfway through our visit, my grandma's mood began to change. The original smile that we'd been greeted with at the door had disappeared, and had turned into a more confused, and stern facial expression. She was obviously tired, so we got her into bed, and covered her with blankets to keep warm. She started looking off into the distance during the end of the visit. As though she was entranced by something, or someone we could not see. She had completely stopped talking to all of us, only reacting with a short "mhm" or a little bit of Italian with my mom. I had the strangest feeling this was going to be the last time I would see her somewhat normal, so before my family and I left, I started saying my goodbyes. I hugged her as tight as I could, and looked her straight in the eyes and said "I love you Nonna". She stared at me, not saying a word, but nodding her head slightly. All I wanted was to hear those words back to me one more time. "I love you Nonna" I said again, with no response. I tried a few more times, but had no luck getting the words out of her. She was too tired and distracted by something. It broke my heart leaving her that day, I knew something was going to change. I never heard her voice after that day, never again getting hear the words she would always say back "I love you too, you be a good boy".

A few days after our visit, my mom received a phone call from my grandma's nursing home. She had suffered 3 seizures in one day, causing her to go into shock. This was the worst news to hear, after getting our hopes up that she had finally gotten better. She was brought back into the hospital, this time in emergency. When we came to see her, she was completely knocked out. Her mouth was filled with blood from a deep gash she gave herself from biting down on her tongue during the seizures. Even in her condition, she still looked good, just unconscious. The doctors informed us that the situation with my grandma was irreversible; she had started down a path she could no longer turn back on. The seizures had hurt her badly, and it was only going to become worse from here. The days following, my grandma began having seizures every 5 minutes. It was the worst thing I have ever witnessed. We would sit all around her as a family, and time out when the next seizure would come, and inform the nurses if anything changed. She eventually had a stroke, and lost the mobility of half her body. She was slowly shutting down, and we could not do a thing about it.

The human body can only go for so long without food or water, due to my grandma's condition, she was not able to swallow anything. Not only was her body shutting down, but was starving to death due to lack of food and liquids. My mom and her siblings were left helpless in the situation. They knew the end was coming, and could not do anything to help my grandma. I told my mom at the very beginning, if there is any point in time where things were going to change for the negative, I wanted to know. If she was going to go, I was going to be right beside her until her last breath. The nursing home called us one day telling us that my grandma had started breathing irregularly, and they feared her time was coming. I got a call from my mom while at work informing me of my grandma's condition. I booked it out of the jobsite I was on, and immediately made my way to the nursing home. I ran to her room to find my family all sitting around her bed, crying, and talking. I thought for sure this was it. The doctors informed my family that it could happen at any time, and for us to prepare. We spent the entire day there, and somehow, my grandma stuck it out. She was one tough lady, stronger than anyone I have ever known.

Life is incredibly weird, and certain events can repeat themselves almost exactly. When my grandfather passed away when I was in the 9th grade, we received a phone call from the hospital at 4 am, informing us that he had a heart attack in the middle of the night. Later on that day, I was picked up from my dad during the lunch hour, and told my grandpa passed away. So, when the day we got a phone call at

4 am once again, but this time for my grandma, I knew this was it.

I remember that morning vividly, I could not sleep for the life of me that night. I was tossing and turning, only catching a few hours here or there. While half asleep, I could hear my mom's voice coming from the kitchen. She was on the phone with my aunt, I didn't need to hear much, just enough to know something was wrong. My dad burst into my room and without a word out of his mouth I said "I'm coming". It was time for us to say goodbye. The nursing home my grandmother lived in was about 20 minutes away from my house. Even with the early morning dead streets, the drive there felt like a million miles away that day. I parked my car and headed for the door just as one of my aunts and uncles were doing the same. No one said much, as we were all deeply involved in our own thoughts. The lights were off in the nursing home, most of the residents were still asleep. We got to her room for 4:30 am, and as I entered the room, a huge rush of sadness over took me. Everyone in my family knew, I knew, this was the last chance we had with her. I sat beside her bed all morning, holding her hand, kissing her forehead, making sure she was as comfortable as she could be. She was completely unconscious, only taking one deep breath every 30 seconds. Her body was shutting down, the breaths we saw her take was her body reacting to not getting enough oxygen, she wasn't doing it on her own.

I watched as my grandma suffered throughout this whole process, and for some reason on this day, she seemed at peace. Maybe it was because the family was all together, maybe it was just her body slowly fading away, all I wanted was her to be free of any more pain. For 3 hours I sat by her with the rest of my family, never letting go of her left hand. The nurses came by and asked if they could change my grandma's clothes, which I thought was pretty pointless. They asked us to step out of the room so they could do what they had to do, which I was never comfortable with. I walked over to a waiting room with 5 of my cousins, my dad and my uncle, and waited. Out of nowhere, another one of my cousins ran into the room "you guys have to come back now!" she hurriedly said. We all ran back into the room, I turned the corner to see the rest of my family who had not joined us in the other room, hugging, and crying. "What's happening?" I asked, looking at everyone completely confused. I turned to my grandma's bed, and saw an image that will forever be burned in my mind. Her body was slouched over, her mouth was wide open, and all colour had disappeared from her face. She was gone. Just like that, I could not believe it. I looked down at her, with tears in my eyes, in complete disbelief. My dad grabbed me and hugged me as tight as he could, my knees were shaking, I could not stop crying. One of the sweetest and most loving people I have ever had in my life, was gone. A very large piece of my heart broke that day.

Throughout this terrible experience, I reflected a lot on my own life. Death is a difficult concept to grasp, and although it is inevitable for all of us, it's something that can be used as a learning experience. While watching my grandmother on her death bed, I wondered how my final moments in life would be. Who would be there to carry on my legacy? Who would be there crying as I said my last goodbyes? What would my legacy be?

All these thoughts ran through my head, I started realizing how much time I had spent staying in the background. When I began going back to school, and not focusing on music, I lost my voice. I started falling into the background of the world, not wanting to be bothered, or bother anyone else. Not living the life I was supposed to, I did not want to be forgotten by anyone, I did not want to be left in the background and left behind. I made it my goal that day to pursue what I wanted in my life, and stop worrying about how others were going to perceive me. The realization came to me that the only way to live my life was to do what I wanted to do, be as happy as I can be, before it's too late. I had let fear stop me from doing things my whole life, and from an early age, I had focused way too much of my energy on how others would perceive me. I had hit a breaking point, I was done feeling scared of being myself while hiding from the world.

This experience was horrible, and not one I recommend anyone goes through. But it was necessary because it taught me many things. When we lose a loved one, we never truly lose them if we hang on to the things that they left with us. The term "they're never really gone" is very true. The legacy they leave behind, and the values and ethics they leave with us, will continue to live through us and our future children and loved ones. My grandma was a very giving woman, someone who I admired tremendously for her hard work, and dedication towards her family. She was always willing to babysit her grandchildren when we were sick, she was always willing to make food for a family get together, she would always be there for a hug, kiss, and the most love she could give. She taught us the value of what true unconditional love was. She was defined by her warm caring nature, and her loving soul. My grandmother taught me the value of being a strong person, even with her struggles in life, she was always willing to push through. Even after multiple surgeries, close calls, and illnesses, my grandmother stuck it out, and did it with a big smile on her face. She treated everyone with respect, and it showed during her final days.

My family and I all stood around her bed when she passed, held hands, and cried. "This is because of her, we're all together because of her" my uncle said.

It was true, and as I looked around the room, I felt so fortunate to have the incredible family that I do. Her legacy was creating a beautiful loving family, teaching us to smile through the tough times, and be as strong as you can possibly be. I am truly thankful to have had such an incredible woman to look up to and remember. We can either be taught something from a bad experience, or we can let it take us down. It is our responsibility to come out of each and every situation we go through, good or bad, stronger and more intelligent. We do not have to let the pain of negativity be carried over to hurt others around us. We were made to grow, and if we are not growing, we are dying. I had many things I wanted to leave behind in this world, and the death of my grandmother was the kick in the butt I needed.

CHAPTER 12

New Beginnings

Each person in this world has something to offer, whether it's a service, a revolutionary idea, or being a loving person. We all have value within us that is sometimes never discovered. Society makes us feel as though we only have value if we own material possessions, get good grades, or win championships. Value does not come from things, it does not come from what costs us money, it comes from what we give back to the world. Value comes from sharing knowledge, sharing our time to make the world better, and giving more of ourselves every day. Too many people live as ghosts in the world, they don't want to be seen, or heard because it can lead to judgment and pain. We cower away from pain using it as a crutch for why we can't do things. Life is not worth a thing if you are not going after what you want every day, and being better for yourself every day.

When I realized I had to become better for myself now, and in my future, my life began to change rapidly. I was always worried about what other people said about me, how they thought of me, how they would perceive me and what I did with my life. But one day, something clicked inside me, a light bulb went off, suddenly I had come to a realization that changed my life entirely. Why do I care about what these people have to say about me, when they don't care about me? Wasting energy and time being hurt, worrying if people will like me, had consumed my entire life. I had focused all my energy on making sure I was not noticed, mocked in any way that would lead to being hurt. People always had an opinion on what I did with my life, and I always cared way too much. The problem with this is, when we focus on how others perceive our life, we take away the focus of what truly makes us happy. We start living our lives based around how others want our lives to be. We no longer live our own life, but instead a life based on the box people have built for us. And that is wrong, for many reasons, and I was so happy to finally come to the realization when I did.

It first started with social media; I never liked how people thought so negatively about the things I posted. I always tried to be the guy that influenced people in a positive or funny way. I love making people laugh, and helping people at the same time. But, I was always met with criticism, painful words from friends who did not care to hear what I had to say. My message of "If I can do it, you can do it" became lost on some people. I used my message in music to try and motivate people to become better versions of themselves, and realize that the goals that they have in life, are just as obtainable as mine were. People took my message wrong, and it made me really sad to see. I never wanted to cause a problem, but drama always seemed to follow me. So, I cut myself off of my social media positive posts for quite some time. Only updating people every now and then on life events, but it was not exciting. It felt like I was going along with what everyone else was doing. Pretending to be happy, so other people would see my life and think "wow, this guy is interesting". The internet is a human highlight reel, designed to show off our best moments, but people don't see the pain behind the scenes. And for me, my pain was a large part of my life, and instead of sharing my experiences to help others, I was hurting in silence.

Silence is deadly, it causes more lost time, happiness, and life, when you are in pain. You feel like you're the only one going through what you're going through, and in turn, become sadder because of that fact. I felt like I had been pushed away from who I really was, and who I wanted to be. When I presented my advice of "Don't let anyone change who you want to be or where you want to go" at my band's CD release, I truly meant it. They were words that came out of me so fluidly as though I knew I needed to hear them myself. Advice I still stand by to this day, because it is a constant reminder of the person I have always strived to be. The person I have worked for years to be, and to become a shining example of. No one could take away my passion, no one could take away my drive to better myself, no matter how many times I may have been knocked down.

Only a short time later, I had forgotten the exact words I had given as advice to myself a few years prior. I let my voice be taken away by the negativity of others. Condescending people, who chose to throw pain my way instead of support, took me down to a level I never wanted to be. The light bulb moment changed this for me, it made me snap out of the negative place I had allowed myself to be. I knew coming back out with my positive outlook posts would ruffle some feathers. Anytime someone does something different than what people know them as, they will be met with some criticism. I knew in my heart, that I had to start doing something better with my time and energy. My grandmother passing away gave me the inspiration to do more, and the pain of being silent for so long, drove me just as much.

There is always value in giving back to the world, and as I have given more of myself, the world has given more back to me. We were never made as people to sit down and shut up. Voices need to be heard, stories need to be told, people need to be listened to. There is strength in sharing pain, there is strength in understanding more about ourselves, and letting go of everything that has weighed us down. Depression comes from struggle, and a lot of it is mental. People feel alone and sad because they feel like they can't talk to anyone, they can't feel ok because they don't know what feeling ok is anymore. I spent many years of my life depressed, not in a suicidal, I don't want to live kind of way. But instead, in a state of low self-esteem and confidence in myself, that wasted many years of my life. The more I have shared my struggles, the more I have realized how truly small those issues were. How silly I was for thinking I was the only person in the world who was going through this, and how much time I had truly wasted being in that state of mind.

People started sharing with me how they appreciated the value I was giving out into the world. I began making videos, posting online, and contributing to blogs; anything to try and send out a message of positivity and motivation to people. I wasn't trying to be someone's guru, I was trying to give advice that I needed to hear, and I wish someone had told me during my struggles in life. We feel misunderstood when we struggle, but by sharing my stories, I began to feel understood. I began to feel like people got me, for once in my whole life. Other people have walked in my shoes, and some have gone through much worse than me. It gave me perspective, and allowed me to forgive my past, and look forward to my future.

The pain we hold onto can be a detrimental thing in our lives, and one we have to come to terms with. By sharing our stories, giving value to others, and allowing ourselves to feel the weight lifted off our shoulders, we become happier. We become more fulfilled and satisfied as human beings when we do not allow our pain to become our crutch, but instead allow it to become our voice to help others that may be going through the same things. That's why sharing your voice is so important and sharing a positive message is so important; it's not for attention, it's to help others who are in need. It may be difficult to go through life alone and no one can get through every challenging hardship in life by themselves. It takes love, guidance, mentorship, and reassurance that everything we are struggling with now, is something everyone has gone through. By seeing people who have struggled doing better for themselves now, we are able to see how we can also change our lives, we will have something to look forward to.

Be a good example of overcoming pain, be a shining light of what pain transformed into strength and prosperity is. Be the strength that others lack, be the mentor that others need, be the dream that others look to have for themselves one day.

CHAPTER 13

Break the Silence

After my grandmother had passed away, as I was stepping away from construction, I had a really reflective moment in my life. I began really starting to look at the things I was doing and figuring out how exactly I was going to leave an impact on the world. How were people really going to remember me.

I was frustrated for a while, trying to figure out my new life path and not having a clue of where to start. The key to life is to make a decision for what you want, and to stick with it. You just have to decide on something, and from that point, the universe and anything else is going to get out of your way. The moment I decided to write this book happened in seconds. I had been researching some of my favorite mentors and speakers and come across one young individual who had written his first book at the age of 14. I watched an interview done by an Australian news channel where he was featured. In this interview, he explains how he just decided one day to write a book, and from that point he wrote and published it in a few months. This was truly inspiring to me, I thought to myself "if he can do it, I can do it too". So, without any hesitation, I shut the video off, and began writing the first draft of this book.

No one ever told me to write my book, no one ever sat down and said "Brysen, you need to write a book because people care". No, it was a desire I had within myself, something that I knew I could have full control over, and accomplish. I didn't allow myself to let the negative thinking of "what if" to stop me. I wanted to create something that left a lasting impression on every single person that read it.

Today I can say, I am happier and more fulfilled than ever before. I trimmed the fat away from my life when it came to negative situations, friends, relationships, and anything else not bringing me value. Is everything perfect all the time? No, and it's not supposed to be. I realized a long time ago that in order for anyone to truly be in a position to succeed in life, they have to be able to know themselves. They have to be willing to fight the world when it's trying to shut you down. I found my voice by expressing myself in a positive way, either through music, or through this book. I stopped allowing the world the opportunity to control me and my emotions. I did not want to live that life anymore, and made a decision to change it. I have worked hard to push through the road blocks, the negativity and frustration, to share with you what I have written.

The lessons I have shared of my life within these pages include many painful memories, and many things I have reflected on while writing this book. I hope anyone who is reading this can really start to see the value in themselves. My hope is that you have started to realize just how powerful your life can be just by taking what you have learned from pain, and creating strength and prosperity. You have tremendous value to offer this world, and no one will see it, until you begin seeing it. No one will believe in you and your dreams until you start believing in it. You cannot, and will not become who you want to be by accident. There is hard work in understanding life, and going through the struggles you need to go through in order to become more successful in whatever it is you want to do.

By finding my voice, I was able to find my confidence, my life purpose, my guidance to fight through every hardship. By staying silent, I hurt myself and wasted my time. Time I could have been using to strengthen people around me, enrich my life and become happier. We have such little time to do what we want to do each and every day of our lives. Why would we ever waste it by letting others take it all away? Why should we conform to become the person everyone else wants us to be, if we are not happy with who we are? As long as we are pushing ourselves to be better, more positive influences, we can in turn start to give more value to others. We are not made to be silent, we are made to give back to the world.

Don't ever let anyone change your opinion of yourself, don't allow anyone to be the overpowering voice for your own life. You're in complete control of what you want to do with your life. No one can take away your inner strength, your ability to think for yourself, to be your own person. Stop worrying about how others will perceive you. No matter what we do in life, there will be naysayers, there will be haters. You will never be able to please everyone, or make everyone like you. Do whatever it is that makes you the happiest in this world. Allow yourself to be happy and truly be yourself. Allow yourself to become the person you were meant to be, by following your passions, following the things that drive you to get out of bed in the morning. When we allow others to control our lives, we allow them to steal our happiness. We allow them to feel powerful over us, to dominate our minds, and our lives. You are stronger than that, you are powerful beyond your imagination, and it takes a sheer force of will and action each day to become whatever it is that you want in life.

Find your voice, allow it to be heard by as many people as you can. Silence only allows pain, silence allows others to keep you in the place they want you. Use your pain to find strength, give that strength back to the world, and allow yourself to become who you were truly meant to be. Allow yourself to be heard, find clarity through making a decision in life to go after one thing and stick to it. Far too many people dabble in too many things, they never stick to one thing long enough to reap the results it may offer. I was a dabbler, someone who always looked for the next best thing to take me where I wanted to go, and in doing so I wasted a lot of time. Do not dabble, make a decision and stick to it, work towards it, die for it. We find clarity through working towards a goal, and not wavering from it.

Remember that patience during this time is the key to becoming stronger as well. You cannot get anywhere in life without first understanding that it will not happen overnight. Each and every attempt at becoming better at something we enjoy doing will push us in the right direction towards success. Whether its success within your job, your family, or anything else, you must fail in order to progress forward in life, you must allow yourself time to grow. Prepare to be in a position of discomfort, and embrace the feeling of the unknown. This time will strengthen you more and more every day.

Your voice is a weapon; it can be used for good or for bad. It can be used to change the world, or help destroy it. You have all the tools necessary to give more than you are, to become more than you are. Do not ever let the world define you. You're the one to decide your own fate.

Find your voice.

Bonus

As a special bonus for readers of this book, I'm offering you access to a special Mini course on "Finding your voice"

To Access this mini course, register your book at www.brysenjohnson.com/bonus

ABOUT THE AUTHOR

Brysen Johnson is a social entrepreneur, speaker, and content marketer from Winnipeg Manitoba. He began his speaking experience as a teenager while performing in local bands, travelling the country and playing to thousands of people. Moving from playing music to sharing an encouraging message of personal fulfillment, Brysen made it his goal to inspire and motivate as many people as possible through his writing, and speaking. Bringing a positive, fresh look to world of entrepreneurship, and creating a stronger generation of millennials along the way.

www.ingramcontent.com/pod-product-compliance
Lightning Source LLC
Chambersburg PA
CBHW032049090426
42744CB00004B/131